Presurgical Psychological Screening
in Chronic Pain Syndromes

♦ ♦ ♦

A Guide for the Behavioral Health Practitioner

Presurgical Psychological Screening in Chronic Pain Syndromes

◆ ◆ ◆

A Guide for the Behavioral Health Practitioner

Andrew R. Block

The WellBeing Group
and
The University of Texas Southwestern Medical School

IEA LAWRENCE ERLBAUM ASSOCIATES, PUBLISHERS
1996 Mahwah, New Jersey

Lawrence Erlbaum Associates, Inc., Publishers
10 Industrial Avenue
Mahwah, New Jersey 07430

Library of Congress Cataloging-in-Publication Data

Cover design by Gail Silverman

Block, Andrew
    Presurgical psychological screening in chronic pain syndromes: a guide for the behavioral health practitioner / Andrew R. Block.
       p. cm.
    Includes index.
    ISBN 0-8058-2407-3 (cloth : alk. paper) ISBN 0-8058-2408-1 (pbk. : alk. paper).
    1. Backache—Psychosomatic aspects. 2. Backache—Patients—Psychological testing. 3. Backache—Surgery—Decision making. 4. Neck pain—Psychosomatic aspects. 5. Neck pain—Patients—Psychological testing. 6. Neck pain—Surgery—Decision making. 7. Chronic pain—Psychosomatic aspects. 8. Chronic pain—Patients—Psychological testing. 9. Chronic pain—Surgery—Decision making. I. Title.
RD771.B217B56 1996
617.5'64'0019—dc20   96-18082
                                  CIP

Books published by Lawrence Erlbaum Associates are printed on acid-free paper, and their bindings are chosen for strength and durability.

Printed in the United States of America
10 9 8 7 6 5 4 3 2 1

To my wonderful family:
Debbie, Aaron, and Stefan
Thanks, again

Contents

Foreword

Dennis C. Turk
University of Pittsburgh School of Medicine

There is a growing body of evidence demonstrating that a substantial proportion of patients who receive surgical procedures for pain-related problems do not achieve satisfactory results. For example, Dvorak, Gauchat, and Valach (1988) reported that at 4- to 17-year follow-ups of patients operated on for lumbar disc herniation, 70% (*n* = 575) of patients still complained of back pain. North, Campbell, et al. (1991) reported that at 5-year follow-up of repeated surgery for back pain, only 33% of cases indicated at least 50% reduction of pain and only about 33% of the patients indicated that they were satisfied with their outcome. The results on functional outcomes are even worse. In an early study, Beals and Hickman (1972) reported that only 36% of industrially injured patients return to work following back surgery. North, Campbell, et al. (1991) reported that only 21% of those who were disabled or unemployed prior to back surgery returned to full-time employment postoperatively. Moreover, in this study, North, Campbell, et al. noted that 14 of 38 patients who were working prior to surgery retired prematurely (before age 60). Thus, the net gain in employment following surgery was approximately 7%. In a 5-year follow-up of patients who had spinal cord stimulators implanted to control back pain, North, Ewnd, Lawton, Kidd, and Piantadosi (1991) reported that only 25% returned to work.

The statistics on the outcome of back surgery are particularly troubling when it is noted that more than 250,000 lumbar surgeries for pain are performed each year in the United States and the costs for such surgeries can be as high as $40,000. Obviously, third-party payers who are approving these surgeries are convinced of a positive outcome, yet the results just cited undermine this expectation in a significant number of cases.

It is important to ask why such a large number of surgical procedures are performed given the relatively modest and even poor outcomes for such a large proportion of patients. Explanations such as the number of surgeons have been suggested as playing a major role in the volume of surgeries. Rates of surgery in different Western countries are also quite variable. For example, patients with back pain are five times more likely to have lumbar surgery in the United States than in England and three times more likely to have back surgery than those in Sweden (Cherkin, Deyo, Loeser, Bush, & Waddell, 1994). There is no reason to believe that the backs of Americans are more fragile than those of people in England or Sweden. Even within the United States, small area analyses have shown that there is tremendous regional variation in the number or surgeries performed (Deyo, Cherkin, Conrad, & Volinn, 1991). There seems to be a direct relation between the number of orthopedic surgeons and the number of surgeries performed (Volinn et al., 1992). This fact should not be especially surprising given the profit motive.

Another explanation provided for the large number of surgeries performed in the United States is the expansion in sophisticated imaging technology. The availability of CAT scans and MRIs permits much better resolution and imaging of anatomical structures. This may be a double-edged sword. The false positive rates for such technological advances is quite high. For example, Boden, Davis, Dina, Patronas, and Wiesel (1990) reported that the MRIs of more than 30% of asymptomatic individuals indicate surgically treatable abnormalities. Conversely, despite these advances, in up to 80% of patients with back pain there are no objective physical findings to substantiate the complaint (Deyo, 1986).

Beyond the question of why so many surgeries are performed in the United States is the question of why the outcomes are not better. It is unlikely that the competence of the highly trained orthopedic and neurosurgeons is sufficient to account for the outcome results cited.

There has been an accumulating body of evidence demonstrating that the relation between physical impairments, pain, and disability are relatively modest. For example, Waddell (1987) reported that the correlations between impairment and pain, impairment and disability, and pain and disability were .27, .51, and .31, respectively. Disability, the individual's response to structural pathology, is obviously affected by factors other than the pathology per se.

A growing number of studies have appeared in the literature attempting to identify the best predictors of long-term disability following an injury. Most of the research has focused on work-related injuries. A wealth of evidence has demonstrated that physical pathology actually pays a relatively minor role in predicting disability. Rather, psychological (e.g., substance abuse, reinforcement of disability by families), sociodemographic (e.g, pending legal actions associated with disability claim), and job-related (e.g., job dissatisfaction) factors appear to be of much greater significance in predicting return to work following work-related injuries (Bigos et al., 1991; Gatchel, Polatin, & Mayer, 1995; Klenerman et al., 1995). Psychosocial factors have also been shown to be important predictors of response to surgery (Love & Peck, 1987).

Third-party payers have become aware of these data and are beginning to challenge surgical interventions and many now require second medical opinions. A more recent development is the requirement for presurgical psychological evaluation. The nature of the psychological evaluation that should be performed remains, however, rather vague. Third-party payers who request a psychological evaluation may assume that there is a standard assessment battery. This is actually not the case. Most psychologists have used an empirical approach to presurgical screening relying on interviews and the use of whatever assessment instruments they have experience with and with which they are most comfortable. The efficacy of a standard assessment battery has not been empirically established nor is there consensus among behavioral health professionals.

In this important volume, Dr. Andrew Block provides the rationale for a systematic protocol for presurgical screening for chronic pain syndromes. Dr. Block is eminently qualified to serve in this capacity, as he has extensive experience as a behavioral heath practitioner who has performed hundreds of presurgical assessments. Moreover, he has conducted research in the area of chronic pain and thus has an appreciation for the importance of establishing an empirical basis for use in clinical decision making. Dr. Block's approach to presurgical screening builds on both his clinical and research background and his extensive knowledge of the relevant research literature.

The two greatest advantages of this volume are the research basis for the proposed protocol and the practicality of the recommendations. Dr. Block has created a detailed but user-friendly model for presurgical psychological screening that is readily accessible to behavioral health practitioners even if they have little background in chronic pain or experience in presurgical screening.

In this volume, Dr. Block not only provides a detailed assessment algorithm and decision-making strategy, he also acknowledges the impediments to successful completion of presurgical psychological screening. For example, patient resistance is a major issue in presurgical psychological screening and the presence of an adversarial relationship can impede the screening process and undermine the development of appropriate recommendations. Dr. Block appropriately identifies this topic and provides detailed recommendations and guidelines as to how resistance should be addressed in order to prevent conflict.

Most importantly, Dr. Block provides a context in which the presurgical psychological screening is conducted. He emphasizes the importance of awareness on the part of the behavioral health practitioner that psychosocial screening is only one aspect of the surgical decision-making process. The behavioral health professional needs to be cognizant that he or she is serving as a consultant and that the results of the presurgical psychological screening must be viewed in the larger perspective of the decision to proceed or withhold surgery.

Dr. Block provides a detailed strategy for behavioral health practitioners in which biomedical information is integrated with the psychological assessment. Practical methods for assessment and the integration with biomedical information are covered in depth. Specific rules and an algorithm for decision making and recommendations are provided.

The importance of communication both with the patient and the referral source should not be minimized. Dr. Block emphasizes how the results of the presurgical psychological screening can be communicated effectively and efficiently both to referring surgeons and patients. In presurgical psychological screening, the behavioral health practitioner serves in a consultative role. It is essential that the information provided in reports to referring surgeons be clear, concise, and make specific recommendations regarding appropriateness for surgery, alternatives, or complementary treatments. This volume contains detailed information regarding not only what to communicate but how to communicate in order to produce the greatest impact.

It is evident throughout this volume that Dr. Block has worked in the trenches. He is authoritative in his discussion of the issues and methods associated with presurgical psychological screening. Readers will obtain a real sense of not only how to work with the patients being screened but also how to operate within the health care system and the surgery context.

Careful examination of this volume and the incorporation of the guidelines presented should enhance the credibility of the behavioral health care practitioner. With the growing evidence for the role of psychological factors in response to surgery and disability and the acceptance of this by third-party payers, presurgical psychological screening can expand the role of the behavioral health practitioner. This challenging role can significantly increase the opportunities for behavioral health care professionals within the evolving health care system.

I highly recommend this volume. It is surely the most comprehensive and practical approach to the topic of presurgical screening that I have encountered. Carefully following the guidelines established by Dr. Block should go a long way toward providing patients with approach alternatives or complementary treatments and ultimately improving surgical outcomes.

References

Beals, P. K., & Hickman, N. W. (1972). Industrial injuries of the back and extremities. *Journal of Bone and Joint Surgery, 54A*, 1593–1598.

Bigos, S. J., Battie, M. C., Spengler, D. M., Fisher, L. D., Fordyce, W. E., Hansson, T., Nachemson, A. L., & Worthly, M. D. (1991). A prospective study of work perceptions and psychosocial factors affecting the report of back injury. *Spine, 16*, 1–6.

Boden, S. D., Davis, D. O., Dina, T. S., Patronas, N. J., & Wiesel, S. W. (1990). Abnormal magnetic-resonance scans of the lumbar spine in asymptomatic subjects. *Journal of Bone and Joint Surgery, 72A*, 403–408.

Cherkin, D. C., Deyo, R. A., Loeser, J. D., Bush, T., & Waddell, G. (1994). An international comparison of back surgery rates. *Spine, 19*, 1201–1206.

Deyo, R. A. (1986). The early diagnostic evaluation of patients with low back pain. *Journal of General Internal Medicine, 1*, 328–335.

Deyo, R. A., Cherkin, D., Conrad, D., & Volinn, E. (1991). Cost, controversy, crisis: Low back pain and the health care of the public. *Annual Review of Public Health, 12*, 141–156.

Dvorak, J., Gauchat, M. H., & Valach, L. (1988). The outcomes of surgery for lumbar disc herniation. I. 4–17 year follow-up with emphasis on somatic aspects. *Spine, 13*, 1418–1422.

Gatchel, R. J., Polatin, P. B., & Mayer, T. G. (1995). The dominant role of psychosocial risk factors in the development of chronic low back pain disability. *Spine, 20*, 2702–2709.

Klenerman, L., Slade, P. D., Stanley, I. M., Pennie, B., Reilly, J. P., Atchison, L. E., Troup, J. D. G., & Rose, M. J. (1995). The prediction of chronicity in patients with an acute attack of low back pain in a general practice setting. *Spine, 20*, 478–484.

Love, A. W., & Peck, C. L. (1987). The MMPI and psychological factors in chronic low back pain: A review. *Pain, 28*, 1–12.

North, R. B., Campbell, J. M., James, C. S., Conover-Walker, N. K., Want, H., Piantadosi, S., Rybock, J. D., & Long, D. M. (1991). Failed back surgery syndrome: A 5-year follow-up in 102 patients undergoing repeated operation. *Neurosurgery, 28*, 685–691.

North, R. B., Ewend, M. G., Lawton, M. T., Kidd, B. H., & Piantadosi, S. (1991). Failed back surgery syndrome: A 5-year follow-up after spinal cord stimulator implantation. *Neurosurgery, 28,* 685–692–699.

Volinn, E., Mayer, J., Diehr, P., Van Koevering, D., Connell, F. A., & Loeser, J. D. (1992). Small area analysis of surgery for low-back pain. *Spine, 17,* 575–581.

Waddell, G. (1987). A new clinical model for the treatment for low-back pain. *Spine, 12,* 632–644.

Preface

In 1975 I had the opportunity to become a technician in a new type of program being formed by the Dartmouth Medical School's Department of Psychiatry. This "Behavioral Medicine Unit" was designed to treat the emotional problems experienced by patients with medical illnesses. It was through this program that I first became acquainted with patients having chronic pain syndromes. During my graduate training, chronic pain patients, as well as their spouses, became the subject of my doctoral dissertation. I continued working with chronic pain patients after obtaining my doctoral degree, until 1987, when I began working with The Spine Institute in Indianapolis. At this facility, Dr. John Begin, an orthopedic surgeon, first asked me to psychologically evaluate a spine surgery candidate, in order to render an opinion as to the patient's suitability for invasive treatment. Even though the patient had a clearly ruptured disc, Dr. Begin suspected that the patient was so depressed that he might not respond well to surgery. I performed this evaluation by drawing upon my knowledge of general chronic pain syndromes. Thus began my explorations into what is becoming a burgeoning application of behavioral medicine—presurgical psychological screening (PPS).

At the present time, PPS is recognized by a number of insurance companies and even state Worker's Compensation systems, as being a significant component of the evaluation process for patients with chronic pain. These third-party payers, acknowledging the cost-effectiveness of PPS, readily authorize such evaluations. In some cases, PPS is even required for chronic pain patients. Even though I am obviously elated with such growing acceptance of PPS, I am somewhat surprised by it, in view of the fact that there are no texts that spell out in specific detail how to conduct

PPS and reach valid conclusions. This practice guide attempts to fill that significant void.

This text presents a comprehensive approach to PPS in chronic pain syndromes. It is designed to provide any behavioral health practitioner, as well as the trainee, with both scientific knowledge of the basis of PPS, as well as many hands-on techniques. This practice guide also contains a number of forms and session outlines that can be directly utilized, or that can be altered to fit the reader's needs. Furthermore, the text provides models for identifying and combining risk factors for poor surgical outcome, so that one can reach valid and reliable predictions of surgical results.

I have attempted, throughout the text, to present all scientific research on which the critical decision points in PPS are based. In addition, the text provides a number of clinical suggestions, based on my experience with more than 500 PPS procedures, which may augment both the information-gathering and the decision-making process. The text also provides outlines for psychological interventions that can facilitate surgical outcome, as well as those that may stand as alternatives to invasive treatment.

A large portion of this practice guide focuses on one specific syndrome: chronic back pain. There are several reasons for this focus. First, by far the majority of PPS studies have been conducted on this population. Second, back pain carries the highest economic and social costs of all chronic pain syndromes. Third, my own experience is more extensive with spine pain patients than with other pain syndromes.

PPS in back pain patients can serve as a model for screening in other pain syndromes. I have attempted to develop such a model in chapter 8, by extending PPS to chronic pelvic pain and temporomandibular joint dysfunction. The text, then, culminates in a general model that can be used in screening across a wide range of chronic pain syndromes.

Although I have attempted to ground the text firmly in research it contains many of my own opinions. Some of these will undoubtedly be proven wrong and others may be substantially altered as the field of PPS grows. The text is best viewed as one practitioner's perspective on a field that is in its early stages. It is my hope that this practice guide will not only contribute to the acceptance of PPS, but may also serve as a starting point to demonstrate both its scientific validity, as well as its value to the patient, the physician and the insurance industry.

Acknowledgments

I have been fortunate throughout the years to be associated with a number of supportive and insightful colleagues. Many of them contributed to the development of this volume. Three orthopedic surgeons, John Begin in Indianapolis, Howard Cotler in Houston, and Richard Guyer in Plano, were particularly influential in starting me on the path of PPS. I am especially grateful to Dr. Guyer for reviewing the medical components of this volume. Most of my work in evaluating spine pain patients has been performed at the Texas Back Institute. I would also like to thank several other surgeons at this facility for their support, including Stephen Hochschuler, Ralph Rashbaum, Alexis Shelokov, Scott Blumenthal, John Peloza, and John Regan.

Many of my ideas about PPS were developed through discussions with other behavioral health providers. I especially appreciate the contributions of psychologists John Riley, David Hanks, Martin Deschner, Rafael Sacasa, and Kyle Babick. Diane Lokay-Nickel, Cindy Pladziewicz, and Jodi Glass added many insights through our discussions of patients and reviews of drafts of the manuscript. Elaine Wacholtz and Deanne Ware provided invaluable assistance in tracking down references and producing the bibliography for this text.

The original impetus for this book was provided by Dave Roble and Ray Deveaux, both of whom are with National Computer Systems. Their support and encouragement through early stages of the manuscript development was invaluable.

In developing the material included in chapter 8, I received invaluable assistance from Dr. Gerald Ballard, Dr. Donna Massoth, and Dr. Robert Reiter.

Early drafts of this manuscript were reviewed by several psychologists, including Frank Keefe, Ed Kremer, John Reeves, William Deardorff, and Dennis Turk. I am very grateful for their comments and insights. Two of these individuals, Ed and Frank, have been my mentors, both during my education and throughout my professional career. I will be forever grateful to them for their guidance and insight in examining chronic pain patients.

—*Andrew R. Block*

Chapter 1

Introduction and Overview

Presurgical Psychological Screening in Chronic Pain Syndromes

Pain is an unfortunate daily experience for many individuals. Chronic pain, lasting 6 or more months, is suffered by approximately 30% of the U.S. population (Bonica, 1990). These individuals wake up, function during the day, and go to sleep trying to keep pain at a minimum while, at the same time, maintaining some quality of life. They may be frequent visitors to the doctor and the pharmacy. When they find relief it is usually short-lived and comes at a cost, such as dependence on narcotic medications or complete limitation of activity. Pain often becomes the central point of their existence.

All pain is disturbing, irritating, and distracting, but when it is experienced on a constant basis, these noxious characteristics can become intolerable. Individuals who experience chronic pain can become increasingly physically disabled and emotionally distraught. Depression, and even suicidal thoughts, may arise. Marriages may disintegrate and jobs may be lost. The suffering individual is, therefore, willing to spend tremendous amounts of time and energy in order to eliminate or reduce the experience of chronic pain.

The general pattern of pain treatment takes a fairly predictable course. Usually, when pain is first experienced, initial diagnostic and intervention efforts are minimal, and may be limited to medication, rest, and reassurance. Most often this is sufficient, and the pain may pass in a few days or weeks. If the pain persists, more expensive diagnostic tests, such as magnetic resonance imaging (MRI), computerized axial tomography (CAT) scans, and the like, may be used. Correspondingly more intense and expensive treatments, such as injections, chiropractic, and physical therapy, may be taken. However, after many months and treatments, some patients still feel little or no relief. There may then come a point where the patient may think: "If only someone could cut out the source of the pain I would be happy." Thus, the groundwork is laid for considering surgery as a solution to the pain.

Chronic pain can be experienced in almost every organ system of the body. It is associated with a huge range of physical diagnoses (Merskey & Bogduk, 1994). In many of these conditions, invasive treatment may be a plausible approach to removing the physical source of the pain, or at least reducing its impact on the patient. Thus, surgery may offer the possibility of reduced suffering, improved independence and quality of life, and a return to greater functional ability.

Research suggests, however, that surgery for chronic pain relief requires a great deal of circumspection. Chronic pain is not simply a result of an untreated physical condition. Rather, psychological factors also play a large role in chronic pain. Patients may have long-standing psychological problems, predating the pain, that can influence their pain perception and the ability to handle the chronic pain condition. Also, psychological and interpersonal difficulties may be experienced in response to the pain, worsening its impact. Thus, chronic pain can be viewed as a syndrome in which physical and psychological factors interact to affect the outcome of any intervention. Surgical success or failure may be determined by this complex interplay.

Failure of surgery for relief of chronic pain can have serious consequences. Often, failed surgery may produce iatrogenic effects, such as the development of scar tissue, nerve damage, or weakening of physical structures. Further, the patient may be more functionally disabled or require more narcotic medication than prior to surgery. Sometimes the initial surgery may only represent the beginning of a long trail of expensive, invasive interventions, providing little or no pain relief. Thus, the failure of surgery can place extreme burdens on the patient, the medical community, and the insurer who pays for treatments.

This practice guide describes an approach to psychological evaluation of the chronic pain patient who is being considered for surgery. This approach, termed *presurgical psychological screening* (PPS), uses interview and testing techniques to identify emotional, behavioral, and psychosocial difficulties that have been demonstrated to negatively impact surgical outcome. This PPS approach emphasizes the importance of examining such psychological factors in the context of both the patient's specific physical condition, as well as the proposed surgery. Thus, the interaction of medical and psychological factors is explicitly considered in each case.

The PPS approach described in this volume has two goals. First, the patient is given a surgical prognosis; good, fair, or poor pain relief is expected as a result of surgery. Thus, PPS can serve to sharpen the surgeon's diagnostic accuracy, screening out those patients who are likely to respond poorly to surgery. Second, a set of treatment plans is developed to augment surgical outcome or as pain control alternatives to surgery. Thus, PPS may facilitate the surgery in producing greater pain relief and may reduce treatment time and cost. Further, in cases where invasive treatment is not advisable, PPS can provide techniques for pain control and improvement in function, which are both less costly than surgery and do not run the risk of iatrogenic difficulties.

The bulk of this practice guide is spent examining PPS for chronic back and neck pain patients. By far, the majority of PPS research has been performed on these populations. Carefully examining PPS for spine surgery allows it to stand as a more general model for PPS. Psychological factors observed in chronic back pain are also found frequently in other pain syndromes. In the final chapter of this volume, psychological factors are examined in two additional pain syndromes that are frequently treated with surgical intervention: chronic idiopathic pelvic pain (CPP) and temporo-mandibular joint dysfunction (TMD). The final chapter builds on the findings in these pain syndromes to develop such a general PPS model, which can be used in screening surgical candidates who have a wide range of chronic pain syndromes.

Chronic Back Pain

Back pain is one of the most vexing problems in health care today. It affects approximately 70% of all individuals in the United States at some time during their lives (Fordyce, Brockway, & Spengler, 1986) and is the second most frequent cause of visits to physicians (Cypress, 1983). Back pain is the leading cause of disability and lost production in the United States (Loeser, Bigos, Fordyce, & Violinn, 1990). The direct and indirect costs of low back pain alone are estimated to exceed $50 billion per year in the United States (Frymoyer, 1991). Yet, the most effective course of treatment for an episode of back pain is often to perform no medical or surgical intervention. In fact, most of those affected can recover with just 2 to 3 days of bed rest and anti-inflammatory medication (Deyo, Diehl, & Rosenthan 1986).

Not all back pain sufferers recover so easily. In the desperate search for relief, some patients go on to a wide variety of treatments. This small number of patients both incur tremendous medical expenses and experience protracted frustration. By way of illustration, S. Leavitt, Johnson, and Beyer (1971) found that 25% of patients with job-related low back injuries are responsible for 87% of total treatment costs. Similarly, Spitzer (1987) found that 7.4% of all industrial back claims were responsible for 86% of total costs. It is most likely in response to such recalcitrant patients that a number of specialized interventions have developed or flourished, including chiropractic, biofeedback, acupuncture, and work hardening, among others. Although all of these treatments may provide relief, some patients continue to suffer. These are often individuals who are eventually considered for spine surgery.

According to Spitzer (1987), only about 1% of back pain sufferers require surgery. Yet this still represents a huge number of patients . A recent survey by Taylor, Deyo, Cherkin, and Kreuter (1994) indicates that 279,000 operations for low back pain were performed in the United States during 1990, with the number of surgeries continuing to climb. The largest proportion of these surgeries were for herniated discs. About 16% involved spinal fusions. For these surgical patients, the only solution has been to remove or repair the offending body part—the putative "pain generator."

Unfortunately, spine surgery often does not have the desired effect. For example, Dzioba and Doxey (1984), in examining the outcome of 116 occupationally injured lumbar surgery patients, found that 43% had poor results and 50% had good to excellent results. Weber (1983), in a randomized study of 126 back pain patients, found no major differences between conservatively treated and operated patients. Turner et al. (1992), reviewing published research on spinal fusion surgery outcome, found that satisfactory clinical outcome is obtained in 65% to 75% of patients, depending on the type of fusion performed. Similarly, a literature review on lumbar discectomy (Hoffman, Wheeler, & Deyo, 1993) found a mean "success rate" of 67%. Thus, even with the development of highly sophisticated diagnostic procedures, and with constant improvements in surgical techniques, the cure for many cases of back pain remains elusive.

The uneven results of spine surgery may be explained by any number of factors. Perhaps adequate diagnostic tests are not always performed, or improper surgical techniques are used (S. Walker & Cousins, 1994). It may be the case that some surgeons are simply better technicians than others. However, there is a large body of research suggesting that the variability in spine surgery outcome may at least be partially explained on the basis of psychological factors. Emotional condition, personality, environmental factors and reinforcers, it would appear, exert strong influences on pain perception and response.

Psychological Influences on Spine Surgery Outcome

The earliest investigations relating psychology and spine surgery outcome were conducted by one of the most respected orthopedic surgeons in the United States, Leon Wiltse (Wiltse & Rocchio, 1975). The original study examined a relatively simple surgical procedure, chemonucleolysis, a technique that involves chemical ablation of a ruptured disc nucleus. This study assessed psychological status using the Minnesota Multiphasic Personality Inventory (MMPI). These researchers found that "symptomatic success" of chemonucleolysis was obtained in 90% patients having low scores on the MMPI hypochondriasis (*HS*) and hysteria (*Hy*) scales, compared to a 10% chance of success in patients with high scores on those two scales. As in most presurgical screening research, all patients in this study had identified physical pathology to account, at least partially, for their complaints. Wiltse concluded that "a given patient's response to pain is very much a psychological phenomenon ... (even) if the patient has objective findings which justify surgery, arrangements should be made for psychological counseling before and after surgery" (p. 482). He further stated that "If the patient has unfavorable findings by psychological testing ... and few objective findings, the surgeon should be very slow to resort to surgical treatment, since the symptoms are not likely to be relieved." Thus, for Wiltse, spine treatment success was a matter of assessing and appropriately treating both the physical and psychological problems experienced by the patient.

A more recent example of presurgical psychological screening is that of Spengler, Ouelette, Battie, and Zeh (1990). This study carefully assessed medical and some psychological factors in patients undergoing elective lumbar discectomy. All patients were examined for neurological signs and other physical signs, and they received diagnostic tests such as lumbar myelography or CT scans. In addition, all patients were administered the MMPI. Clinical outcome was measured in terms of pain relief, improvement in functioning, and reduced use of narcotics. Results showed that clinical outcome was much more strongly predicted by psychological than by medical factors, although the most powerful predictive model combined both factors. As in the Wiltse study, elevated MMPI *Hs* and *Hy* scores were strongly associated with poor outcome. Spengler et al. (1990) concluded that "differences in pre-morbid psychological factors may be meaningful contributors to the variations in (the treatment of lumbar disc herniation)" (p. 236).

Numerous additional studies have been conducted examining psychological influences on the outcome of various spine surgery procedures (see Block, 1992, for a review). In addition to chemonucleolysis, studies have been conducted on spinal fusion, discectomy, spinal cord stimulators, and other invasive treatments. These studies are extensively reviewed throughout this practice guide. As is seen, such studies demonstrate that failures of spine surgery can be predicted by considering the patient's medical problems in combination with psychological and other emotional factors.

Presurgical Psychological Screening

This volume details PPS, an approach that identifies and quantifies risk factors associated with poor surgical outcome in order to render a decision concerning surgical prognosis. PPS is based on a thorough understanding of research literature combined with guided clinical insight. PPS, as described herein, has an additional goal—the development of psychological treatment plans for either facilitating surgical outcome, or as alternatives to surgical intervention. Such treatment plans address the identified risk factors, in order to reduce the patient's suffering and achieve maximum functional gains, while avoiding medical treatments with a high likelihood of failure.

Like any psychological evaluation, PPS requires the behavioral health practitioner to use interview and testing techniques in order to identify mental health-related diagnoses and to develop any necessary interventions. However, because PPS is directed at addressing the specific question of surgical outcome it involves procedures (e.g., reviewing medical records) that are not normally a part of a psychological evaluation. Furthermore, performance of an accurate PPS requires that the behavioral health practitioner be able to draw on or have specialized knowledge of psychological and medical risk factors for poor surgical outcome.

PPS involves the following procedures:

1. Review of medical records.
2. Semi-structured interview to identify surgical risk factors.
3. Observation of pain-related and other behaviors.
4. Psychological testing to identify additional risk factors.
5. Determination of surgical prognosis.

6. Suggestions to facilitate surgical outcome or alternative treatment plan.
7. Preparation of PPS report.

In order to perform a thorough and accurate PPS, all of these procedures should be completed. The following chapters address each of these procedure in turn.

The ultimate goal of the PPS is the determination of surgical prognosis. This determination must be at once, both succinct and scientifically justifiable. As far as the surgeon is concerned, the most effective means of communicating the results of PPS is to give a clear, unambiguous result: The client is expected to have a good, fair, or poor surgical outcome.

Of course, reaching a decision about surgical prognosis is a complicated process, involving both scientific knowledge, judgment, and clinical experience. It is based on integrating all of the information gleaned from the medical records, interview, observation, and testing. Following the procedures just listed allows the practitioner to reach outcome predictions and develop treatment plans with confidence and scientific validity.

Risk Factors for Poor Surgical Outcome

The PPS determination of surgical prognosis rests on the identification of risk factors falling into two domains: psychological and medical.

Psychological Risk Factors. As has been noted, a great deal of research is currently underway relating psychological factors specifically to the outcome of spine surgery, and , more generally, to the outcome of pain treatment. Some of the major factors that have been investigated are listed in Table 1.1. Examination of these risk factors, and techniques for eliciting them, constitute a large portion of this text (see chapters 4 and 5).

The psychological risk factors listed in Table 1.1 are primarily identified through the interview, behavioral observation, and psychological testing procedures. Some of these factors can or must be identified using multiple procedures. For example, depression can be identified through psychological testing (such as the MMPI), interview, and, to some extent, through observation. Substance abuse may be identified through review of medical records and through interview or testing. When possible, one should make use of all the possible techniques to assess each risk factor, for the convergence between evaluation techniques leads to more certainty about conclusions.

TABLE 1.1

**Major Psychological Factors Influencing Spine Surgery
and Pain Treatment Outcome**

Reinforcers for Injury

    Receipt of worker's compensation

    Pending lawsuits and application for disability payments

    Job dissatisfaction and anger at employer

    Heavy job demands

    Reaction of spouse to injury and marital dissatisfaction

Historical Issues

    Physical and sexual abuse

    History of substance abuse

    Past history of psychological difficulties

Personality

    MMPI scale elevations

    Hy, Hs elevations (pain sensitivity)

    D scale elevations (depression)

    Pd scale elevations (anger and authority problems)

    Pt scale elevations (agitation and worry)

Cognition

    Coping skills

    Low self-reliance

    Low pain control

In this volume these psychological risk factors are viewed as additive. That is, the greater number of these risk factors identified in a particular case, the poorer the expected outcome. As is seen in the course of the text, some of these risk factors have stronger scientific support and, therefore, should be given greater weight in the determination of surgical prognosis.

Medical Risk Factors.   Even in the absence of a PPS, the decision to perform spine surgery is never simple. Surgeons are acutely aware of the variable outcome of surgery. Furthermore, the medico–legal context of the decision to operate is always in the back of their minds. Surgeons are subject to lawsuits for both deciding to operate on certain patients, as well as deciding not to operate. Additionally, the pathophysiology (or tissue damage) underlying the patient's pain complaints may not be entirely clear. Finally, the probability of good outcome may vary with the type of surgery planned.

The following is a list of the medical risk factors that have been associated with poor outcome of spine surgery:

1. Chronicity of pain complaints.
2. Multiple previous spine surgeries.
3. "Destructiveness" of the surgery.
4. Nonorganic (symptom magnification) signs.
5. Heavy, nonspine-related, prior medical treatment.
6. Smoking.
7. Obesity.

Within the context of PPS, these risk factors are primarily identified through review of the medical records, or through interview with the referring physicians. Methods for identifying these risk factors are discussed in chapter 3. The medical risk factors are considered additive, with a higher number of risk factors associated with poorer surgical outcome.

Outcome Category Definitions. Predicting surgical outcome requires the establishment of concrete definitions of success and failure. Although many such definitions exist, the majority of well-conducted research studies use some variation on the criteria established by Stauffer and Coventry (1972; see Block, 1992, for a review). These criteria, which form the outcome prediction categories used in this volume, have been revised by Turner et al. (1992):

Good Outcome: pain absent or occasionally mild, able to work at usual job, and minimal or no activity restrictions.

Fair Outcome: mild persistent or occasional moderate pain; able to work and perform most normal activities, but with some restrictions.

Poor Outcome: persistent moderate or occasional severe pain, with little or no pain relief from surgery, or severe activity restrictions.

It may appear that these outcome prediction categories oversimplify the desired results of spine surgery. After all, the experience of protracted spine pain may lead patients to experience many additional difficulties. Some of these problems include loss of income, disruption in family and marital relationships, emotional instability, decreased self-esteem, and heavy dependence on medical providers. However much one may hope that spine surgery brings about a resolution in many of these problems, such a desire is probably unrealistic. After all, many of the problems experienced by back pain patients may preexist any spine injury. For example, many spine surgery candidates have a history of early childhood abuse (Schofferman, Anderson, Hinds, Smith, & White, 1992). Also, preinjury psychiatric diagnoses and drug dependency are seen rather frequently among these patients (Polatin, Kinney, Gatchel, Lillo, & Mayer, 1993). The experience of back pain may exacerbate preexisting emotional or behavioral difficulties associated with such problems. Perhaps the best that can be expected for such patients is that spine surgery may reduce some of the excessive distress associated with prolonged pain and disability, thereby allowing the patient to return to preinjury levels of psychological functioning. Thus, the definition of *good* surgical outcome may vary widely, depending on the patient's preinjury level of emotional and behavioral functioning.

The PPS Model

The determination of surgical prognosis requires the clinician to evaluate the patient for both psychological and medical risk factors. Once these are identified, the clinician must make a leap from the data obtained during the PPS to a decision on surgical prognosis. It must be determined whether the level of risk on each of these dimensions is sufficient to declare that the patient has poor surgical outcome prognosis.

There are a number of ways in which the data obtained during PPS can be combined to predict outcome. The integration approach of this practice guide begins with the recognition that the pain experience is most effectively viewed as an interaction between physical and mental events. Objectively observable medical phenomena are to some extent separable from the subjective, self-reported measures gathered by the behavioral health practitioner. For this reason, determination of surgical prognosis may be inferred from the level of risk on both the psychological and medical constructs. It is only when both the mental and physical aspects of spine pain are problematic that the patient can be determined to have a poor outcome prognosis.

Another way to view this decision-making process is consider a two-dimensional risk table, as in Fig. 1.1. Surgical prognosis follows from the four possible combinations of medical and psychological risk factors. Those patients with minimal risk in both domains are determined to have a good prognosis. Those who have both a high level of medical and psychological risk are declared to be poor surgical candidates. Those who have a high set

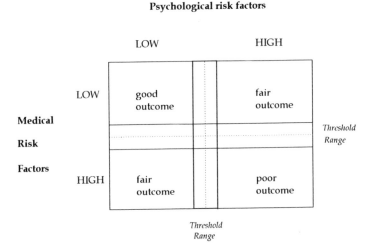

FIG. 1.1   Surgical prognosis determined by medical and psychological risk factors.

of risk factors on one dimension and a low set of risk factors on the other fall into the fair prognosis group. It is this group of fair risk candidates who represent the greatest clinical challenge.

The simplified 2 X 2 risk table in Fig. 1.1 requires the clinician to determine whether the level of both psychological and medical risk exceed a "high-risk threshold." The threshold for each dimension represents a conceptual watershed, a dividing line between those expected to do well and those expected to do poorly in recovering from surgery. In many cases, determining the proper placement of the patient relative to the threshold is easy. This occurs when the patient is either at a very high or very low level of risk. In such cases, determination of surgical prognosis may take little clinical skill. It is when the patient presents a mixed picture that determination of risk level becomes more difficult.

In the cases of patients having moderate risk levels, the expertise of the evaluator becomes extremely important. In such cases, one needs to draw on three important sources of information. First, the clinician must be well versed in scientific research on the medical and psychological factors affecting surgical outcome. These are discussed in chapters 3, 4, and 5. Second, the clinician must have established rules for determining when enough of these risk factors exist to declare that the patient carries a high level of psychological or medical risk. Suggested rules are given in chapter 6. Finally, in cases of mixed risk, the clinician must apply experience and judgment to more subtle information derived from the interview in order to determine proper placement relative to the high risk threshold. Such subtle information and decision points are discussed throughout the text, and are summarized in chapter 6.

Expertise in PPS allows the evaluator to walk a fine line, primarily tying the decision on surgical prognosis to data, while tempering the decision with clinical judgment. The databased decision making is critical. Without scientific justification, the decision on surgical prognosis may come to be based more on intuitive feelings of the clinician. Such feelings may be quite counterproductive to the PPS process. The spine surgery candidate often presents very differently from the psychotherapy candidate. Spine surgery candidates have physical problems and often see no reason for a psychological evaluation. Thus, they may be very guarded or even openly hostile, and little rapport may develop. Ordinarily, such a patient might be seen as a poor psychotherapy candidate. However, defensiveness, anger, and poor rapport with the therapist do not make the patient a poor surgery candidate. It is the combination of identifiable risk factors with clinical expertise that determines surgical prognosis.

Prognostic and Treatment Recommendations

PPS serves much broader functions than simply giving a surgical prognosis. It is not enough to simply state that the patient is expected to have a good, fair, or poor response. Rather, the clinician must also use the information obtained in the PPS to determine whether there are ways to improve outcome, or whether surgery should be avoided altogether. In fact, placement in a particular prognostic category leads to some general treatment recommendations. These general types of recommendations are listed in Table 1.2.

Examination of Table 1.2 reveals important aspects of PPS. First, by placing the patient in a specific prognostic category the clinician is recommending a course of action concerning surgery. When a patient is given a good prognosis, the clinician is recommending that the surgery be performed. When a fair prognosis is obtained, the clinician feels there are a fairly high number of risk factors, some of which may be reduced through treatment. This psychological intervention may be conducted either preoperatively (in which surgery may be delayed), or postoperatively. With a poor prognosis the clinician has determined that surgery is not a wise option and should be avoided.

TABLE 1.2

Recommendations Resulting From PPS

Good Prognosis—Clear for Surgery

    Recommend means to facilitate surgical outcome

    Recommend postoperative psychological intervention

Fair Prognosis—Clear for Surgery, With Additional Recommendations

    Recommend compliance measures

    Recommend preoperative psychotherapy

    Recommend consideration of psychotropic medication

    Recommend reduction of substance use

Poor Prognosis—Do Not Operate

    Recommend alternative treatment approaches

    Recommend discharge plans

Examination of Table 1.2 also reveals that once the prognostic category is determined, recommendations are given for procedures to improve outcome or clarify the patient's status. As can be seen, even for patients who are at minimal risk of poor outcome (i.e., in the good outcome category) the PPS can reveal ways to facilitate response to surgery. Such facilitative recommendations would minimize any risk factors identified and capitalize on the patient's strengths. For example, the clinician may determine that the spouse tends to reinforce pain behavior or disability by providing the patient with a great deal of attention for pain complaints. Thus, one might recommend including the spouse in treatment planning. Similarly, the PPS can determine if the patient will benefit most by detailed explanations of the surgery, or alternatively, if the patient should be given simple information and treatment recommendations. The PPS may also reveal issues requiring postoperative psychotherapy in order to maximize improvements.

For patients in the fair prognostic category, the treatment recommendations are even more critical. In the fair prognosis category, the number of risk factors identified is significant. Psychological interventions should be recommended to deal with those modifiable risk factors identified. For example, a patient who is overusing medications may be required to sign a medication contract, identifying the specific plans for reduction of narcotics in the postoperative period. Similarly, the clinically depressed patient may be placed on antidepressant medications prior to undertaking surgery.

For patients in the poor prognostic category the PPS may become the primary source of alternative treatment plans. The clinician should devise a program for maximizing improvements in a patient who has been declared unsuitable for surgery. Such plans will aim to capitalize on the patient's strengths and to reduce problematic behaviors that limit functional ability or promote sensitivity to pain.

Detailed treatment planning for patients in the three prognostic categories is given in chapter 6.

Red Flags

Clinical judgment and expertise are important in one other way for PPS. There are times when the clinician must suspend, at least temporarily, a focus on surgical prognosis and, instead, call an immediate halt to a proposed surgery. This occurs when the clinician identifies a crisis situational "red flag." These red flags include active suicidal ideation, active psychotic process, active high level of narcotic or street drug use, and extreme negative attitude about surgery. Identification of a red flag does not mean surgical clearance is impossible. Rather, these patients must be considered on temporary hold until the crisis situation is resolved.

Summary and Conclusions

Physicians have come to an increasing recognition of the role played by psychological factors in pain perception and response to treatment. Recent research demonstrates that such emotional and behavioral factors can also predict the outcome of spine surgery. For these reasons, both surgeons and the insurance industry are beginning to request that many spine surgery candidates undergo presurgical psychological screening.

PPS is multistep process. The first step involves the identification of risk factors for poor surgical outcome. Medical risk factors are identified through a review of medical records, and by conversing with the physician or staff. Psychological risk factors are identified through an interview, behavioral observation, and psychological testing. Once all risk factors have been elucidated, they are integrated to determine the patient's overall surgical prognosis: expectation of good, fair, or poor outcome. Clinical expertise allows the evaluator to balance identified risk factors with professional judgment in order to reach this final conclusion. Differing treatment recommendations follow from these three outcome prognoses.

Although the development of standards for PPS is in its infancy, the body of research on the combined influence of medical and psychological factors in affecting spine surgery outcome has had a profound effect on surgeon's orientation toward the evaluation of surgical candidates. In the literature, one frequently encounters statements extolling the importance of PPS. For example, Schofferman (1995) stated that, "It is essential to gain some degree of psychologic insight about the patient ... since it is so well established that psychologic issues are critical to recovery from painful disorders of the spine" (p. 58). An even stronger proponent of psychological evaluation has been Nachemson (1992), editor-in-chief of the orthopedic journal *Spine*, who stated that in considering spine surgery, "Clinical studies with good control and nonbiased follow-up examinations have demonstrated that psychologic factors need be [*sic*] addressed more thoroughly than hypothetical physical problems or biomechanical factors" (p. 16).

One is certain of the acceptance of a new diagnostic or treatment technique when it gains recognition by insurance carriers. Thus, it is of significance that indemnity and worker's compensation insurance are beginning to include psychological screening in their evaluation regimens. For example, Eker and Wiseman (1994) recommend PPS for spine fusion candidates, stating that "a substantial literature demonstrates the importance of psychological factors as predictors of outcome following back surgery." Similarly, the Texas Worker's Compensation Commission (TWCC) recently accepted "Peri-Operative Mental Health Evaluation" as a standard procedure prior to spine surgery (TWCC, 1995). Finally, in my own recent clinical experience there have been a number of incidences wherein private insurance companies have required spine surgery candidates to undergo a PPS. Thus, third-party payers are recognizing that PPS can lead to improved overall treatment outcome and also, by avoiding potentially unsuccessful surgery, to cost savings.

Thus, PPS is quickly becoming an area that is attracting a great deal of attention from clinicians, researchers, and insurance companies. Like any area undergoing rapid development, the opportunities to demonstrate the value of PPS are becoming plentiful. On the other hand, without generally accepted evaluation measures and techniques, PPS may lose its validity, and, therefore, its credibility. It is the aim of this practice guide to provide a standardized objective PPS procedure, based on scientifically validated psychological and medical predictors of spine surgery outcome.

Chapter 2

Pain Theories

Presurgical psychological screening represents a new extension of a long line of theory and research concerning the nature and treatment of pain. For many decades it has been recognized that pain is a complex phenomenon, involving "affective, cognitive, and behavioral as well as sensory mechanisms" (Fields, 1991, p. 8). However, there have been a number of quite disparate viewpoints on the processes involved in pain perception and response. This chapter represents a brief review of four major theoretical viewpoints that have had a significant influence on the field of pain management. It is not critical to understand these viewpoints in order to perform PPS. Thus, the reader who wishes to quickly gain knowledge of PPS techniques may skip this chapter and return to it at a later time. However, knowledge of the major theories on pain will help the behavioral health practitioner to develop and refine his or her own conceptualization of pain mechanisms. Further, scientific research can spring from an understanding of pain theories. Finally, the information discussed in this chapter will help the practitioner to communicate with other professionals in the field of pain management.

Theories on the psychology of pain share many central concepts. All begin by recognizing that subjective pain sensations are initiated when there is an injury to some physical structure. Thus, psychological theories generally agree with Chapman's (1978) definition that, "pain is an unpleasant, subjective experience that occurs when tissues are damaged or stressed" (p. 169). There is also general agreement that the subjective experience of pain, and the effect of the pain on the patient's behavior, can be influenced by nonphysiological events. Such events, which may be emotional, interpersonal, developmental, and/or environmental, fall under the general umbrella of psychological factors. Finally, there is widespread agreement that psychological treatments can reduce pain sensation and improve the lot of many suffering patients.

On the other hand, the psychological theories on pain diverge in a number of areas. First, there is some disagreement as to the relative role of psychological factors in the etiology of pain. As is seen here, some assume that pain must begin with tissue damage. For these theories, the process of *nociception* (i.e., stimulation of neurons sensing physical damage to body structures) is a necessary precondition for the experience of pain. From other perspectives pain can be purely "psychogenic." That is, it can arise from psychological events unrelated to actual physical injury.

Theories on the psychology of pain also differ on two other points. There is a wide divergence of opinion on the specific nature of nonphysiological events assumed to influence the experience of pain. Differing relative emphasis is placed on the role of environmental events, psychological defense mechanisms, attention, and developmental processes. Finally, the types of psychological treatments purporting to alter pain experience are disparate, ranging from uncovering of repressed memories and traumatic events, through pain-coping strategies and hypnotic pain control techniques, to systematic reinforcement of nonpain-related "well behaviors."

This chapter explores some of the major concepts articulated by major psychological theories on pain. This presentation is neither exhaustive, nor does it review in depth critical evidence for or against particular pain theories. Rather, this chapter allows readers to compare and contrast theoretical conceptualizations in order to discover their relative value in understanding the spine pain patient.

Psychoanalytic Viewpoint

The first modern works on the psychology of pain examined pain from a psychoanalytic perspective (see Gamsa, 1994, for a review of the history of psychological factors in pain). One can find very early psychoanalytic references to pain in the writings of Sigmund Freud (Breuer & Freud, 1895). Freud took a "dualistic view" of pain. He saw pain as stemming either from primarily organic or mental causes. That is, for Freud, tissue damage was not a necessary precondition for pain. Pain sensations could be purely psychogenic.

In discussing his early case of Elisabeth Von R, Freud drew this mind–body distinction quite clearly:

> A patient suffering from organic pain, if it is not accompanied by any nervousness, will be able to describe it definitely and calmly; it may perhaps be lancinating, appear at certain intervals, and extend from this to that location. ... The neurasthenic [a hypochondriac with anxiety neurosis] in describing his pain gives the impression as being occupied with some difficult mental problem, something far beyond his powers. His features are tense and distorted ... he rejects all designations that the physician makes for his pain. ... He is ostensibly of the opinion that language is too poor to give expression to his feelings. These sensations are something unique, they never existed before. ... (p. 39)

Elizabeth Von R was an "hysteric" patient, who had a 2-year history of leg pains. In early childhood, she had an actual physical problem, rheumatism, which could have accounted for her leg pain complaints. However, as an adult, the rheumatism was no longer present. Freud used this case to demonstrate the central psychological process that he believed was involved in pain perception. Freud believed that many patients with psychogenic pain suffer from intense unconscious anxiety arising from early developmental conflicts. The pain symptom, then, became a way to resolve this anxiety and to restore some semblance of psychic balance.

In the case of Elizabeth Von R, Freud believed conflicted anxiety had a basis in an early erotic attraction for her brother-in-law. He states,

> As a result of this conflict, the erotic ideas were repressed ... and the affect connected with them was utilized in aggravating or reviving a simultaneously (or somewhat previously) existing pain. It was, thus, the mechanism of a *conversion for the purpose of defense*. ... (p. 44)

The concept of *conversion* is central to the Freudian viewpoint on psychogenic pain. Conversion involves changing psychological conflicts into physical symptom complaints. Conversion allows the psychological conflict to be repressed into the unconscious, where it can cause the patient no further conscious emotional distress. However, by repressing psychic energy, conversion maintains the pain symptom long after any physiologic basis for the pain is resolved.

The treatment for psychogenic or hysterical pain involves undoing the conversion, allowing the patient to become aware of repressed conflicts through the process of psychoanalysis. As Breuer and Freud (1895) stated, "individual hysterical symptoms immediately disappear ... without returning if we succeed ... in thoroughly awakening the memories of the causal process with its accompanying affect, and if the patient ... (gives) verbal expression to the affect" (pp. 59–60).

Psychoanalytic concepts have spawned a large body of research. In 1959, Engle published a significant, widely cited psychoanalytic paper on the "pain-prone patient." He again emphasized the role of conversion in the etiology and maintenance of pain complaints. Another significant early study was that of Hanvik (1950), who reported on the use of the MMPI in evaluating back pain patients. He found that, compared to patients with "organic" pain, those with "functional" pain (i.e., those with "no clear-cut organic findings") had higher scores on many MMPI scales, including Hy, Hs, and several others. This study seemed to confirm that deep-seated psychological conflicts could lead a patient to experience protracted, unexplainable pains.

The Hanvik and Engle papers led to a flurry of "dualistic" research studies. Such research separated the origin of pain into two categories: physical or psychogenic (Elkins & Barrett, 1984; Freeman, Calsyn, & Loucks, 1976; see Keel, 1984, for a review), drawing distinctions between patients with these two types of pains. However, many in the field now reject psychoanalytic concepts because the theory on which they are based is untestable. It is difficult if not impossible to prove the existence of early childhood conflicts and of the conversion of these conflicts into physical pain. On the other hand, psychoanalytic concepts, such as "hysteria," "functional pain," and "conversion" continue to be widely used in discussion of pain patients.

Behavioral Perspectives

A somewhat different perspective on the role of psychological factors in assessment and treatment of pain came from Fordyce's (1976) pioneering text, *Behavioral Methods in Chronic Pain and Illness* (see also Fordyce, 1978). Fordyce's perspective grows out of operant learning theory, as articulated by Skinner (1938, 1974).

According to this behavioral perspective, tissue injury is a necessary precondition for pain perception. Fordyce (1978) stated, "There is, as a starting basis, nociception ... defined as 'potentially tissue-damaging thermal or mechanical energy impinging on specialized nerve endings' ..." (p. 52). The nociceptive process is seen as likely to cause the patient to emit some overt behaviors indicative of the pain, such as moaning, limping, rubbing the injured body part, and so on.

In the case of acute pain, such overt pain behaviors are viewed as "respondents," which can be simplified to mean that they are essentially reflexive actions in response to tissue damage. As pain persists, such overt, respondent pain behaviors inevitably produce certain responses by the patient and the social environment. Family members may rush to give the patient medication, the employer may give the patient time off from work with pay, or the patient may receive narcotic medications. These responses to the patient's pain displays can have the effect of turning the "respondent" acute pain behavior into "operant" chronic pain behavior.

Operants are overt actions that are "sensitive to the influence of consequences" (p. 55). All operants increase in frequency if followed by reinforcing consequences, as is the case when a dog is rewarded by food for raising his paw in response to a specific command word. Overt pain behaviors can become operants like any other behaviors, and may be expected to increase in frequency and intensity to the extent that reinforcing consequences follow their presentation.

For Fordyce, the rewards contingent on pain behaviors control their presentation. The direct and indirect rewards, in fact, may be sufficient to produce pain behaviors, "long after the original nociceptive stimulus has resolved" (p. 59). If the patient further receives little reward for alternative well behaviors—if he or she is ignored when feeling good, or actually prevented from increasing activity—the result can be increasing disability, medication dependence, and weakness.

Early research based on Fordyce's operant conceptualizations supported this perspective. Cairns and Pasino (1977), for example, applied behavioral techniques to the treatment of back pain patients. These patients were rewarded with praise from staff members for increases in a specific exercise, such as walking around a track, but they did not receive praise for another exercise, such as riding a stationary bicycle. Results showed that back pain patients displayed increases in physical exercise only when they received attention and praise for such improvements. No change occurred when the exercise was not praised. In a somewhat related application of the behavioral approach, several studies (Block, Kremer, & Gaylor, 1980a; Lousberg, Schmidt, & Groenman, 1992; Turk & Rudy, 1988) found that some actions by a spouse, such as giving the patient medication in response to pain complaints, may "reward" pain behavior, increasing the patient's tendency to display such behavior.

Fordyce's operant approach to pain management provided the springboard for the development of pain centers. In pain centers, the patient is often evaluated and treated by a team of clinicians, including physicians, psychologists, counselors, physical therapists, exercise physiologists, and occupational therapists. The general approach of the pain center is that pain behaviors are to be treated by systematic alterations in contingent reinforcement. Well behaviors are rewarded with praise, and even concrete reinforcers such as money, athletic shoes, and so on. Pain behaviors are ignored. Pain centers also work with the employer and significant other to help them minimize reward for pain behavior. Pain centers have generally shown that even many highly resistant patients can show improvements in pain relief and can increase functional ability through an operant approach (Block, 1982; see Flor, Fydrich, & Turk, 1992, for a review).

The behavioral perspective on pain remains quite influential. This is perhaps because, unlike the psychoanalytic perspective, many behavioral concepts are clearly testable. For example, as shown by Cairns and Pasino (1977), one can demonstrate that the systematic application of contingent reinforcement can lead to a decrease in pain behavior and an increase in well behavior. However, it should be seen that the behavioral perspective has much similarity to the psychoanalytic. The respondent–operant distinction of the behavioral approach is not unlike the organic–functional distinction posited by Freud and his followers. Further, both perspectives include a reinforcement mechanism for nonorganically based pain. For the behaviorist the rewards are that "good things happen when I hurt ... (and) ... bad things don't happen which otherwise would" (Fordyce, 1978, p. 59). From the Freudian perspective, pain is reinforced primarily through avoidance of unpleasant affect. Thus, it may well be that the main strength of the behavioral perspective is not its unique validity or insight, but its ability to generate scientifically verifiable hypotheses.

Cognitive Perspectives

The cognitive perspective is the third set of psychological theories on pain. Cognitive theories grow out of the substantial psychological literature on coping with stress (Lazarus & Folkman, 1984). According to cognitive perspective, pain begins with physical stimulation of damage-sensing neurons (nociception, as previously noted). However, the relationships of nociception to pain perception and to pain behaviors are strongly influenced by the ways in which the patient mentally processes these aversive signals. If the patient thinks about and copes with the pain signals in appropriate ways, a sanguine result can be obtained. On the other hand, an individual who focuses excessively or unnecessarily on pain sensations can magnify their impact.

One example of the power of cognitive processes to affect the experience of pain is found in research on attentional control. *Attentional control* refers to cognitive strategies that may lead the patient to focus on, or be distracted from, pain sensations. A number of studies have shown the intensity of the pain experienced in laboratory experimental pain studies can be diminished by distraction instructions (Blitz & Dinnerstein, 1971; Grimm & Kanfer, 1976; for reviews see ; Eccleston, 1995; Fernandez & Turk, 1989). Such instructions might include focusing on pleasant events, relaxation training, or thinking of other activities. Distraction under hypnosis has also been shown to be effective in reducing clinical pain (Hilgard, 1978). Erickson (Rossi, Ryan, & Sharp, 1983) provided a good description of hypnotic distraction techniques:

> You can use hypnotic dissociation to indirectly induce an anesthesia for patients. ... Just have them move to another part of the room, leaving their pain where they were. ... Don Colcum, an obstetrician, likes to send his patients down to the ocean to watch the waves and the seagulls while he works on their bodies back in the delivery room in Bangor, Maine. When it is time, the patients come back from the seashore and he shows them their babies! (pp. 233–234)

Clinicians and researchers have defined a wide variety of processes involved in the cognitive response to pain signals (see Jensen, Turner, Romano, & Karoly, 1991a). Some of these processes, such as positive outcome expectancies and strong beliefs in one's ability to control pain, are associated with better overall emotional adjustment and improved functional ability in chronic pain patients. Others, such as cognitive errors like *catastrophizing* (the belief that things will get worse and worse), tend to lead a pain patient into a downward spiral of increasing pain and decreasing ability (see chapter 5 for further review of cognitive factors in pain).

Many chronic pain treatment programs now include explicit training in cognitive pain control techniques. Such techniques include hypnosis, rational-emotive therapy (Ellis, 1962), reframing (Lankton & Lankton, 1983), and many others. Further, studies have shown that improvements in the status of chronic pain patients are associated with the development of positive cognitive changes (Jensen, Turner, & Romano, 1994).

The power of cognitive therapy techniques in affecting improvements for chronic pain patients, as well as the intuitive appeal of a cognitive perspective, have led to a proliferation of assessment devices and cognitive treatment techniques. This very explosion of the cognitive perspective presents a number of problems. As has been noted by Fernandez and Turk

(1989), as well as Eccleston (1995), there is currently considerable confusion about several issues in the cognitive perspective. Cognitive terminology is not consistent. Eccleston pointed out that in one study a treatment strategy is labeled *somatization,* whereas in a second study the same treatment strategy is referred to as *dissociation.* Further, in many research studies it is unclear whether positive cognitive changes cause or result from improvements in the status of chronic pain patients. Nonetheless, the cognitive perspective has firmly established itself as a significant influence on the field of pain management.

Integrative Perspectives

The theories discussed so far in this chapter all focus most of their attention on psychological mechanisms involved in pain perception and response. These theories spend little time considering the physiological underpinnings of pain. That is, while they recognize, to a greater or lesser degree, the role of nociception in initiating the pain experience, they give short shrift to the physical mechanisms involved in transmission and perception of pain signals. These theories focus instead on explanations of how psychological events lead to variations in the perception and effect of pain signals, once these signals arrive at the brain.

Integrative theories do not have these limitations of the other theoretical perspectives. Integrative theories begin with an understanding of the physiological mechanisms by which tissue damage is monitored, and the neuronal signals indicating tissue damage are transmitted to the brain. Integrative theories go on to include consideration of psychological mechanisms, but within a physiologic framework. Emotional, cognitive, and environmental factors are postulated to affect the physical transmission of pain signals. Some of these psychological events can have an inhibitory effect of the transmission of signals, whereas others may increase signal transmission. The heuristic value of integrative models is that they are able to incorporate a wide range of physical and psychological research on pain into a single and relatively simple model of pain.

In 1965, Melzack and Wall proposed the theory that has had the most significant effect on the entire field of pain research and current clinical intervention. This perspective, termed gate control theory (Fig. 2.1), is a conceptual model that recognizes that pain responses result from an interaction of physical pain signals with sensory, motivational, and cognitive factors. According to gate control theory, pain begins with nociception, the stimulation of nerve endings sensing tissue damage. The theory proposes that there exists a physical "gate" in the dorsal horn of the spinal cord (the area where peripheral nerves enter into the cord). In order for pain to be perceived and pain responses generated, a large number of pain signals must pass through this gate and trigger (T) impulses to be transmitted upward through the nervous system.

   According to this theory, the spinal cord gate is thought to be influenced by two types of neural events. First, the interaction of different types of peripheral nerves appear to affect the gate. Certain neural input to the gate, particularly through large diameter, fast-moving (L) fibers is seen to close the gate, whereas input from small diameter, slower moving fibers (S) opens the gate. Neural input concerning tissue damage is normally carried along both types of fibers. Thus, the first signals of damage arriving at the gate, along the L fibers, would tend to close the gate, inhibiting pain perception. This may explain why one often does not initially sense pain in response to an injury, such as a burn or cut. However, once slower moving input along S fibers reaches the gate, it opens, allowing pain signals to be transmitted upward. Thus, pain is subjectively experienced.

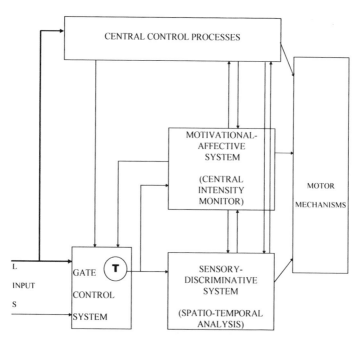

FIG. 2.1.   Gate control theory (based on Melzack & Dennis, 1978).

A second, and very different mechanism, is thought to also affect the spinal gate. This mechanism involves neural influences from a "central control process." Such central processes are the "brain activities subserving attention, emotion and memories of prior experience" (Melzack & Dennis, 1978, pp. 5–6). Gate control theory proposes that these central control processes send neural signals from the brain, down the spinal cord to the gate, and influence the extent to which the gate is open or closed. Certain thought processes, such as anxiety or fear may act in such a descending fashion to open the gate, whereas other cognitive activity, such as distraction, may selectively close the gate. Thus, one may experience severe pain with minimal nociception, or little pain with intense tissue damage, depending on the context of the injury, prior experience, and one's emotional state.

Gate control theory recognizes that pain modulation occurs not only at the spinal gate, but also at higher levels of the nervous system, including the brainstem, thalamus, and cerebral cortex. At these higher levels, cognitive, motivational-affective, and sensory-discriminative factors interact in response to pain signals arriving through the "ascending" nervous system to the brain. It is this interactive response that finally determines the ways in which the individual perceives and acts when experiencing pain.

Gate control theory has several advantages over more purely psychological theories. First, it incorporates scientifically proven knowledge of the physiological processes involved in pain. Further, it provides a physiological explanation for the effects of psychological events on pain perception and response. Psychological events are seen to open or close the neural gates affecting the transmission of pain signals. Finally, gate control theory generates hypotheses concerning pain modulation that can be objectively tested.

Gate control theory has been the impetus for a number of developments in pain treatment. For example, medical pain control devices, such as transcutaneous electrical nerve stimulators (TENS) units, have been developed that are designed to close the gate through stimulation of L fibers and the activation of descending inhibitory influences. Further, generalized multidisciplinary programs draw heavily on the integrational approach of gate control theory. Finally, this theory has given birth to the biopsychosocial model, now widely considered the most appropriate approach to understanding pain.

The biopsychosocial model (Fig. 2.2; Loeser, 1982) is a somewhat simplified version of gate control theory. Both perspectives view nociception as the starting point for a series of internal and external events, culminating in overt behaviors. Within the biopsychosocial model, the first step in this process involves the translation from nerve impulses to pain perception. This step is influenced by both physiologic mechanisms of pain signal transmission, as well as cognitive factors involved in sensory integration and interpretation. The next step involves the patient's experience of suffering, an experience relating to the meaning of the pain, that can be affected by a host of emotional, personality, and interpersonal factors. The final step in the biopsychosocial model is the display of "pain behaviors." Such overt manifestations of injury are the end result of the interaction of multiple physiological, psychological, and social factors.

The conceptual biopsychosocial model considers the experience of pain as an ever widening series of circles (Fig. 2.2). The model implies that the impact of an injury or tissue damage can grow as the process moves from nociception to pain behavior. Similarly, perception of the pain signals may be distorted so that the pain may seem to be magnified. The patient's suffering may be disproportionate to nociceptive input and pain perception. Finally, the behavioral expression of the injury may be so excessive that it dominates the patient' life. All along the way, the interaction of physical and psychological factors influence the pain process, determining the extent to which the patient's life is disrupted by the injury or disease process.

The biopsychosocial model strips gate control theory of many of its theoretical underpinnings. It is essentially a pragmatic approach to examining the pain process. Its focus is on those factors that affect pain perception, suffering and behavior, rather than postulating specific pain theories. Thus, the biopsychosocial model is broad enough to encompass both

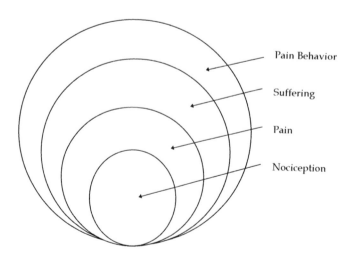

Pain Behavior

Suffering

Pain

Nociception

FIG. 2.2.   The biopsychosocial model: A conceptual model of pain (based on Loeser, 1982).

research on specific physiological pain transmission mechanisms (such as those postulated by gate control theory), as well as strictly psychological research (guided, for example, by behavior theory). In fact, all research examining influences on the process of pain perception and response can be incorporated into this model. Furthermore, psychological and medical factors affecting the outcome of pain treatment can be investigated without regard to theories or philosophical implications. The only requirement of treatment, as guided by the biopsychosocial model, is that it leads to a reduction in the overall pain experience and pain behavior.

The biopsychosocial model is a useful one for PPS. Certainly, all spine surgery candidates have tissue damage to at least partially account for their symptoms. Thus, nociception is the starting point for their pain experience. However, according to this model, psychological factors should influence both the impact of the injury on the perception and experience of pain, as well as the patient's response to treatment. In the end, positive surgical outcome should result from a reduction in nociception (through removal or treatment of damaged tissues) in combination with clinical attention to the many issues, both psychological and otherwise, that create high levels of pain behavior and suffering. Thus, this model provides for a truly "holistic" approach to the assessment and treatment of pain.

Summary

Theories on the psychology of pain have had a profound impact on the development of PPS techniques. In this chapter, four major theoretical perspectives were identified. The psychoanalytic approach emphasizes the role of conversion of unconscious anxiety into physical symptoms and pain complaints. The behavioral approach places emphasis on environmental responses to pain behavior that act through reinforcement to increase the likelihood of pain displays. The cognitive perspective examines the role of attention, coping and pain beliefs in determining the patient's perception of and response to pain. Finally, the integrative models of gate control theory and the biopsychosocial model view pain behavior and suffering as resulting from an interaction of physical and psychological mechanisms. By understanding these four perspectives the behavioral health practitioner can appreciate the techniques involved in PPS at a deeper and more critical level.

Chapter 3

Obtaining Medical Information

The behavioral health practitioner who would provide PPS services is venturing into territory that is far from the usual course of psychological training—the highly technical world of spine surgery. In order to be successful, the practitioner must acquire a whole new set of practical and clinical skills. First, the practitioner must be able to develop referral mechanisms so that physicians understand why, when, and how they should refer the patient. Next, PPS requires one to have a least a basic level of medical knowledge concerning the spine, common spine problems, diagnostic procedures, and surgical techniques. Also, the practitioner needs to have a base of scientific information about medical risk factors for poor surgical outcome so that these can be gleaned from medical records and integrated with the psychological information obtained during the PPS. This chapter provides the practical, conceptual, and empirical information necessary to interact with physicians and to aid practitioners in understanding their decision-making process.

The Referral Process

An effective PPS begins long before the patient enters the office of the behavioral health practitioner. It begins when the practitioner establishes a relationship with the referring physician. The practitioner needs to explain the PPS process to the physician, including its potential value to both the patient and to the physician. The physician needs to know how to make referrals and how to get the desired information back from the practitioner. By carefully developing the referral process, the practitioner ensures that the PPS can be most effective and accurate. There are several steps that should be taken to establish and expedite appropriate referrals.

Suggestions for Optimizing PPS Referrals

Discuss Benefits of PPS With the Surgeon. Surgeons are trained to identify and repair tissue damage. They have little or no formal training in mental health. Yet they often implicitly or explicitly recognize two facts. First, they are aware that many of their patients have emotional or behavioral problems. Second, they have a wealth of experience demonstrating that psychological factors have affected the outcome of their procedures. Obtaining referrals from surgeons, then, becomes a matter of heightening their awareness of these facts and providing information on the benefits of PPS. In discussions with a potential referring physician it should be pointed out that PPS can:

- Improve their overall outcome by identifying potential nonresponders.
- Improve outcome in surgical cases by individualizing treatments based on the patient's psychological characteristics.
- Reduce average treatment cost and duration by avoiding ineffective procedures.
- Reduce number of problem patients.
- Identify patients with potential for medication problems.
- Provide a psychological diagnosis and appropriate treatments.

Provide Referral Criteria. Not all spine surgery candidates require PPS. Referral sources need to know when a referral is appropriate. It is, perhaps, most effect to provide the physician with a referral criteria sheet (Table 3.1), to be posted in the areas where dictation and prescription writing occur.

Advise the Physician of Appropriate Patient Preparation. One of the most critical features of PPS involves the referring physician's preparation of the patient for this procedure. Confusion, hostility, and defensiveness on the part of the patient can arise if the patient is not carefully informed of the reasons for referral. In making the PPS referral, the physician should inform the patient of the following points:

TABLE 3.1

Referral Criteria for PPS

Exaggerated or inappropriate signs and symptoms of spine injury

Suspected clinical depression or high anxiety level

Severe sleep disturbance

Unrealistic expectations about surgical outcome

High level of marital distress or unexplained sexual difficulty

Poor work attitude or uncertain postoperative vocational plans

Emotional lability or mood swings

Extended period of disability (< 3 months)

Continued use of large doses of narcotics or anxiolytics

Evidence of financial gain or litigation related to spine injury

Referral considerations

0–1 items	Not necessary to refer unless desired by patient
2–3 items	Consider referral for PPS
4+ items	Strongly consider referral for PPS

- The PPS is a mental health (or psychological) evaluation.
- The PPS is a routine procedure, like any other medical test, to assist in developing the most effective treatment plan.
- The PPS is a critical procedure, as important to surgical decision making as any medical test.
- The PPS will help determine if the patient is ready for surgery.
- The PPS can provide an opportunity to discuss emotional, marital, or other injury-related problems being experienced.
- The physician recognizes that the patient has a legitimate injury and that the pain is "real."

Provide Patient Handouts. It is especially useful to provide the physician's office with handouts to be given to the patient who is referred for PPS. An effective handout will help the patient understand and cooperate with the behavioral health practitioner. The handout should describe the evaluation process. The handout should be written in plain language, covering the following points:

- The PPS is a routine procedure for spine surgery candidates.
- The PPS will assist in planning treatments and maximize recovery.

- The PPS will give the patient an opportunity to discuss concerns about many issues including the surgery, work, and emotional issues.
- The PPS is a psychological evaluation involving interview and testing.
- The results of the PPS will be discussed with the surgeon.

In addition, normal issues of confidentiality and cost should be included in this patient handout.

Keep the Referral Process Simple.   Surgeons are very busy and generally do not have time to provide a detailed referral letter. Probably the most effective way to obtain the referral is to provide the physician with a prescription pad bearing the name and address of your practice. List on the prescription pad the types of referrals that may be made, including "Presurgical Psychological Evaluation." At the bottom of the prescription form provide several blank lines on which the physician can write any specific concerns for the patient. However, expect this line will often be left blank by the physician.

Unfortunately, even though the physician may not always provide a rationale for referral, this is often required by insurance companies in order to authorize the PPS. In the case where no referral criteria are provided by the physician, the best approach is to talk to the physician's nurse or assistant, who often knows the patient as well as, or better than, the physician—and certainly will have knowledge of the basis for the referral.

Request Referral as Early as Possible.   The process of identifying the pain generator and determining the need for surgery is not a rapid one. Most often, many medical tests are required, and the patient may visit the physician many times. It is during this work-up phase that the PPS is most effective. The behavioral health practitioner should work with the physician to recognize the presence of symptoms leading to a PPS so that the referral can be made as early as possible. In this way, the PPS has the greatest validity and is most useful to the physician. Once the physician has identified that a patient has a surgical problem, the usual process is to get the patient in for the operation quickly. Requesting a PPS after the surgical decision is made significantly slows down this process, making the physician less likely to refer the patient. Further, at this point the physician often tells the patient that a surgical problem exists. Thus, if a PPS is ordered after the surgical decision is made the patient may recognize the necessity of "passing" the PPS in order to obtain the operation. This may greatly influence responsiveness and presentation during the PPS.

Obtain as Much Medical Information as Possible.   Most behavioral health practitioners do not work closely enough with referring physicians to have access to the complete medical record. Certainly, it is most helpful if all information can be obtained. Absent a complete medical record, the practitioner must obtain at least the following:

- Initial history and physical report.
- Summary of current physical findings and results of medical tests.
- Current prescribed medications and level taken by patient.
- Current medical diagnosis and planned surgery.

Without this minimal information, there is no way to understand the medical risks and problems facing the spine surgery candidate.

Reviewing Medical Records

Understanding the Spine

The goal of the surgeon is to identify the physiologic cause of the pain (the pain generator), and then remove it, repair it, or otherwise limit its effects. This section provides a basic summary of the information likely to be found in medical records. In order to perform the PPS, it is necessary to have a basic understanding of these diagnostic and surgical procedures used by physicians to determine the need for surgery. (For more detailed information see Frymoyer, 1991; White & Schofferman, 1995.)

Basic Anatomical Features of the Spine.   The healthy spine is an amazing structure. It provides support for the body, while also allowing freedom of movement. At the same time, the spine protects and provides a pathway for the spinal cord and its connections throughout the body. Figure 3.1 is a simplified picture of a spine segment, composed of two lower (lumbar) spine vertebrae and an intervertebral disc. As can be seen in this

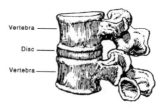

FIG. 3.1. A example of a lumbar spine segment, composed of two vertebrae and an intervertebral disc.

illustration, the major structures of the spine are the bony vertebral body, the intervertebral discs, and the facets, which act as the joints between the vertebrae. An arch (the lamina) in the back of each vertebra, provides a protected pathway for the spinal cord. Ligaments, not shown in the figure, connect the vertebrae, providing it with stability.

Figure 3.2 shows a top (axial) view of an intervertebral disc, as it sits atop a vertebra. Because the discs are much softer than the bony vertebrae, they act as cushions, or shock absorbers, for the spine. Each disc is composed of two sections. There is an inner nucleus, filled with gelatinous material, and an outer ring or annulus, containing much tougher fibers. Nerve roots, attached to the spinal cord, exit between each vertebra, at the foramen, and are connected to various structures throughout the body. Many problems can develop with the discs, as is listed below, leading to referral for spine surgery.

The spine is divided into four sections (Fig. 3.3) containing varying numbers of vertebrae. Each vertebra is numbered. Intervertebral discs are identified by the vertebrae between which they are located. Thus, disc L4–L5, refers to the intervertebral disc located between the fourth and fifth lumbar vertebra.

Spinal Problems

A number of spine problems can develop, leading to referral for surgery. Some of these major problems are listed here:

Bulging Discs: The disc nucleus remains intact but the nucleus and annulus bulge, placing pressure on a nerve root, which causes pain. Bulging discs are common with degeneration—the general process in which the fluid content of the disc is decreased, as a result of aging or trauma.

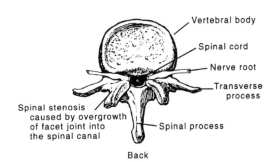

FIG 3.2. Axial (top) view of an intervertebral disc, with spinal cord and associated nerve roots.

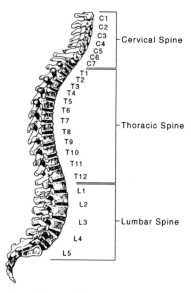

FIG. 3.3. The human spine, with cervical, thoracic, and lumbar areas identified.

Herniated Disc: Similar to a bulging disc, except that the disc annulus ruptures, allowing material from the nucleus to leak through (Fig. 3.4). This nuclear material compresses the nerve root and causes pain. Disc herniations vary from mild, in which leaking nuclear material remains close to the center of the disc, to severe, in which the nuclear material reaches the outer edge of the disc annulus.

Disrupted Disc: A tiny tear occurs in the disc annulus, but the nucleus generally remains intact. Because the annulus contains pain fibers, a torn annulus may cause pain.

Stenosis: Narrowing of the foramen—the pathway by which the nerve roots exit the spine and/or the spinal canal. This usually results when bone spurs (osteophytes) develop, or facets become inflamed, as a result of arthritis. In turn, the nerve roots are irritated, causing pain.

Spondylolysis: Otherwise known as spinal instability. A unilateral defect in the lamina, or bony arch of the vertebra. If present bilaterally, the vertebrae have excessive ability to slide across each other. This puts pressure on the disc annulus, the nerves, the facets, and the ligaments supporting the spine, thus causing pain.

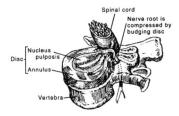

FIG. 3.4. Disc herniation.

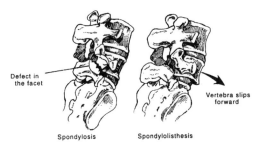

FIG. 3.5. Spondylolysis and spondylolisthesis.

Spondylolisthesis: This is a form of instability, in which there are bilateral spondylolytic defects of the rear portion of the vertebral body, allowing a vertebra to slide forward, out of position (Fig. 3.5). The intervertebral disc, in turn gets stretched. Pain may then arise from the disc, from the cracked portion of the vertebral body, or from pressure on nearby ligaments. The slippage can vary from mild (Grade 1) to severe (Grade 4), in which the veterbral body has slipped far forward of its normal position.

Diagnostic Procedures

Diagnostic procedures are used to determine the cause of the patient's back pain. This search for the pain generator requires two types of evidence. First, it must be demonstrated that the patient has specific objective tissue pathology. Second, it should be demonstrated that this tissue damage is the sole source of pain. Different types of tests are used to satisfy these two requirements. Most often, the identification of tissue damage is accomplished through "static" tests. Such tests use highly sophisticated technology in order to essentially take a snapshot of any tissue damage in the spine. The linkage between tissue damage and pain sensations is often accomplished through a second type of test—a "pain modification" test. In this type of test, procedures are performed that elicit, diminish, or alter the patient's pain perception. The most common types of static and pain modification tests are discussed here. The reader must recognize, however, that new diagnostic procedures are continually developing. The reader is advised to stay abreast of these developments, which are frequently reported the journal, *Spine*.

Static Procedures

X-Rays.   X-rays are usually taken from multiple angles. X-rays are useful for identifying narrowed disc spaces, spondylolysis and spondylolisthesis and, and problems with the facets.

Computed Tomography Scanning (CT Scan).   Essentially a computerized x-ray, CT scans can allow three-dimensional views of the spine. The CT scan can provide good detail about the structure of the veterbrae, as well as soft tissues—the intervertebral discs and nerves.

Bone Scan.   A bone scan is a procedure in which a radioactive calcium is injected into the bloodstream. This material is then absorbed into the bones. This test is especially good for revealing bones that are experiencing rapid growth of cells, such as may occur in vertebral fractures or infections.

Myelography.   Myelography is a procedure in which a water-soluble radiographic contrast material is injected into the sheath covering the spinal cord (the epidural space). This contrast material then flows down the epidural space and around the nerve roots. An x-ray is then taken to observe the flow of the contrast. If the flow down the spinal canal is interrupted, and/or the nerve roots do not fill with contrast material, this may indicate a disc herniation, or other impingement on the spinal cord, such as bone spurs (osteophytes) or spinal abscesses.

Magnetic Resonance Imaging (MRI).   An MRI is a procedure in which electromagnetic fields are passed through the spine. The MRI is less effective than the CT scan at observing bony detail, but more effective for examining soft tissue damage, such as disc herniation or degeneration.

Electromyelogram (EMG).   EMG is a procedure in which very fine wires are inserted into the nerve pathways of the extremities, in order to measure the transmission of nerve impulses. Abnormal results indicate the present of acute or chronic nerve damage.

Pain Modification Tests

Except for emergency situations, spine surgery is elective. It is performed because the patient has intolerable pain that is greatly affecting his or her lifestyle. Because reduction or elimination of pain is the most desired outcome of spine surgery, diagnostic testing should demonstrate that the putative tissue damage is the specific source of the patient's clinical pain. If the relationship between pathophysiology and pain is unclear, the outcome of surgery is, at best, problematic.

Pain modification tests clarify the relationship between identified tissue damage and pain sensation. The first group of these tests, the *clinical pain modification tests* attempt to demonstrate that the tissue damage is the sole source of painful stimulation. Some tests, such as discograms, attempt to aggravate the painful condition, in order to elicit or increase the patient clinical pain. Others, such as facet blocks, attempt to soothe or palliate the tissue damage, in order to demonstrate a reduction in subjective pain sensation.

Nonclinical pain modification tests constitute the second group of tests that explore the relationship of pain to tissue damage. These tests attempt to demonstrate that sources other than the identified tissue damage give rise to the patient's pain experience. This can be done by aggravating areas of the body other than the putative pain generator to see if this elicits the patient's clinical pain, as in the Waddell "nonorganic signs" tests. Alternatively, as in the sequential spinal block, the patient's pain experience can be assessed by blocking the transmission of pain signals along the spinal cord, between the site of tissue damage and the brain. Continued pain in such a situation means that a specific "pain generator" cannot be identified.

The major pain modification tests are discussed here.

Discogram.   This is a clinical pain modification procedure in which radiographic contrast material is injected into the disc nucleus under fluoroscopy. This injection has two purposes. First, an x-ray or post-discogram CT scan of the disc can reveal the nuclear structure. If the nucleus is herniated or degenerated, contrast material can be easily visualized leaking out of the disc nucleus. The contrast material does not leak out of an intact nucleus. Second, the injection of the contrast material acts an irritant, stimulating the patient to experience pain in the same distribution and with same quality as the patient's normally occurring clinical pain. Recent research (Vanharanta et al., 1987) has shown that similar or exact pain reproduction is found upon injection of 93% of herniated discs. Thus, injection of a damaged disc, which reproduces the patient's clinical pain, demonstrates that the disc is the pain generator.

Facet Injection.   A facet injection is a clinical pain modification procedure wherein anesthetic (sometimes mixed with cortisone, an anti-inflammatory) is injected into the facets (joints between the vertebrae), under fluoroscopy. Once the anesthetic is absorbed into the facet, the patient may experience a decrease in pain, identifying the facet as the source of pain. A positive test may be a surgical indication for facet rhizotomy.

Differential Spinal Block.   This procedure is a nonclinical pain modification one in which anesthetic is injected into the epidural space surrounding the spinal cord. This injection is placed above the entry point into the spinal cord of the nerves innervating the area of tissue damage. This anesthetic effectively blocks the transmission of pain signals between the tissue damage and the brain. Continued pain in the presence of this anesthetic indicates that the tissue damage is not the sole "pain generator." There is, at least, an implication that such continued pain must have a psychological basis because the pain source is effectively cut off from the brain.

Symptom Magnification Tests.   Another nonclinical pain modification procedure, symptom magnification tests, were first developed by Waddell, McCulloch, Kummel, and Venner (1980). These tests are a series of symptom magnification assessments, designed to elucidate the presence of nonorganic physical signs in low back pain. These test are performed during the patient's physical examination. There are five different types of test designed to explore inconsistency between tissue damage and pain (see Table 3.2). Positive results in three of the five tests indicate the presence of symptom magnification.

Comment.   There may be two explanations for the uncertain relationship between tissue damage and pain experience. First, the tissue damage identified may not be the pain generator. In other words, some static tests may produce false positives. For example, Barron and Zazandijan (1993) found that MRI identifies disc abnormalities in 40% of asymptomatic individuals. Similarly, Wiesel, Tsourmas, Feffer, Citrin, and Patronas (1984) found that 35% of asymptomatic individuals have abnormal disc findings on CT scan. A second, and probably more far-reaching, explanation for the inconsistent results of these pain modification tests is that the patient's perception of, and reaction to, the pain caused by the tissue damage may be greatly exaggerated or distorted (Block, Vanharanta, Ohnmeiss, &

TABLE 3.2

Waddell's Tests for Nonorganic Signs in Low Back Pain

Tenderness

Superficial—pain in response to light pinch of skin

Nonanatomic—deep tenderness distributed over an area too wide to be localized to one source

Stimulation

Axial loading—Low back pain when pressing on patient's head

Rotation—Low back pain when rotating shoulders and pelvis

Distraction

Straight-leg raising—pain experienced when tested formally but not when tested with distraction

Regional Disturbances

Weakness—"giving away" of muscles that cannot be explained on localized neurological basis

Sensory—diminished sensation to pin prick or light touch in a non-neurological pattern

Overreaction

The observation of excessive verbalization, facial expression, or other overly dramatic behaviors

Guyer, 1996). As is revealed in chapters 4 and 5, this tendency toward misperception of painful stimuli can be elucidated in the PPS. When excessive pain sensitivity occurs, one must assume that even repairing damaged tissues may be ineffective in providing relief.

Surgical Procedures

Once the surgeon identifies the source of pain, surgery may be proposed. Needless to say, surgical technology is constantly changing, with surgeries becoming increasing less invasive and more effective. The behavioral health practitioner is advised to stay abreast of these developments. The major types of surgery in current use are discussed here.

Discectomy. This is a procedure in which the surgeon removes that portion of a herniated disc that is impinging on a nerve root. For most of these procedures, in order to reach the disc the surgeon must first either perform a *laminotomy,* removing a portion of the lamina (the arch of the vertebral body), or a laminectomy, removing the entire lamina. In discectomies, most or all of the disc annulus remains and acts as a shock absorber between the vertebrae. The discectomy can be performed in a number of ways: (a) a standard open procedure, requiring removal or a relatively large portion of the lamina; (b) a less invasive microdiscectomy requiring less removal of the lamina; (c) a less often performed, minimally invasive percutaneous discectomy, in which the disc nucleus is removed by suction through a needle, thus requiring no excision of the lamina. A chymopapain injection may also be used to dissolve the disc nucleus, although the results of this procedure are quite variable. Also, recently developing arthroscopic (endoscopic) discectomy procedures allow the surgeon to view and remove disc material using miniaturized instruments with rigid or flexible fiber optics.

Rhizotomy.   This is a procedure that cuts the nerve pathway from the facet joints. This is accomplished by percutaneously burning the nerves with a radio frequency generator or by freezing the nerves. As a result of this surgery an irritated of damaged facet joint can not transmit pain signals to the brain.

Foramenotomy.   This procedure is performed when the foramen (the passageway for nerves as they exit the spinal column) is narrowed due to stenosis. In this case, the surgeon shaves bony material from the foramen, allowing the nerves to pass through more easily.

Fusion.   Fusion is a procedure performed most often to correct spinal instability (such as spondylolisthesis). This procedure, is also used to correct relatively rare cases of curvature of the spine (scoliosis). In this procedure bone is placed to span the unstable segments of the spine. Eventually, the bones fuse together, stabilizing the vertebrae. The bone used in the fusion is either scrapped off the pelvis (in which case some donor site pain can be expected), or obtained from a bone bank, or both. The fusion can performed on the back of the spine (*posterior fusion*), the front of the spine (*anterior fusion*), or, in very difficult cases, from both the front and back sides (a *circumferential* or *360 degree fusion*). Instrumentation, such as plates, rods, screws, or wires may also be inserted to provide extra stability. A bone stimulator, either implanted into the fusion site, or external dwelling, may be used to facilitate fusion.

Spinal Cord Stimulator.   Also known as a dorsal column stimulator, this is a "salvage procedure" used in the patient who has intractable nerve pain despite multiple previous surgeries. Small electrodes are implanted over the ascending portion of the spinal cord. Electrical impulses, generated by an implanted battery, are delivered to these electrodes, often blocking the transmission of pain signals from the damaged tissue to the brain.

Comment. The behavioral health practitioner may assume that the decision as to the type of surgery proposed is straightforward, with certain positive test findings leading necessarily to specific types of surgery. However, the decision is often not so clear. Various professional groups, such as the American Academy of Orthopedic Surgeons (AAOS) have established clinical criteria for different types of spine operations. However, the value of many of these procedures is uncertain because the only studies supporting them are often retrospective in nature. Thus, the decisions on necessity for and type of surgery are based on many factors, including scientific research, experience, skill, and personal bias. Moreover, each type of surgery presents its own difficulties, carries its own probability of poor outcome, and results in different total health care expenditure. The surgeon must weigh all these and more factors in deciding which type of surgery to perform, and how to perform it.

Medical Factors Predicting Poor Outcome

A number of studies have been conducted to assess medical factors associated with poor outcome. The following represents the major predictive factors identified.

Chronicity. Many authors have posited that the probability of improvement in disability related to back pain decreases with chronicity. Waddell (1987), for example, showed that the likelihood of patient returning to work is 50% at 6 months, 25% at 12 months, and virtually nil if the patient continues to be disabled 2 years postinjury. Junge, Dvorak, and Ahrens (1995), examining discectomy patients, found that patients with poor outcome had longer durations of acute and chronic low back pain, as well as longer duration out of work. Similar results have been obtained by Franklin, Haug, Heyer, McKeefrey, and Picciano (1994) when examining fusion outcome. A review of published fusion outcome research (Hoffman et al., 1993) also identified shorter symptom duration as a predictor of better treatment outcome.

There are several explanations for the negative influence of chronicity on treatment outcome. First, several authors have shown that increasing chronicity leads to a "deconditioning syndrome" (Mayer et al., 1987)—a downward spiral of decreasing strength and physical ability. As patients become deconditioned, they experience greater pain and become more limited in physical strength and endurance, making improvements from any intervention more difficult to achieve. Alternatively, it may be that with chronicity the patient experiences more fear and avoidance or that the incentives for improvement are less. Regardless of the explanation, duration of pain-related disability, especially if more than 1 year, must be considered a risk factor for poor outcome.

Number of Previous Surgeries.   *Failed back syndrome* is a term that describes patients who receive initial back surgery, but have continued intractable pain and functional incapacity (North et al., 1991; Walker & Cousins, 1994). These patients are often later considered for additional surgical treatment. Franklin et al. (1994), for example, found that 23% of patients who underwent lumbar fusion had a subsequent spine operation within 2 years. The Hoffman et al. (1993) review of discectomy research found that approximately 10% of these patients went on to reoperation. Unfortunately, as has been shown by Wadell (1987), the probability of good outcome decreases with each successive surgical intervention. For example, North (1995) stated that "Our overall experience with reoperation has been that the rate of 'success' is approximately one third, and the morbidity significant" (p. 586). Similarly, Pheasant, Gelbert, Goldfarb, and Herron (1979) found that multiply operated patients had a much lower probability of good outcome than did single-surgery patients. Similar findings have been obtained by a number of authors. (Ciol et al., 1994; Franklin et al., 1994; Turner et al., 1992). Thus, previous surgical intervention must be considered a risk factor for poor outcome, with greater risk for increasing number of prior surgeries.

Destructiveness.   All spine surgery necessitates some amount of tissue destruction, in order to reach, and then repair or remove, the pain generator. However, as has been previously noted, spine surgery procedures do not all involve the same level of tissue destruction. Some procedures (e.g., microdiscectomy, arthroscopic and percutaneous discectomy, chymopapain injections, and rhizotomy) can be considered "minimally invasive." Other procedures, particularly decompression and fusion, involve greater destruction. The destructiveness of the fusion varies with the number of levels involved, whether hardware is used and with the type of fusion. A circumferential fusion, of necessity, involves more tissue destruction than either an anterior or posterior fusion involving the same number of levels.

It is difficult to compare outcome studies between surgeries with different levels of destructiveness. For example, Turner et al. (1992) reviewed 47 articles reporting on treatment for herniated discs, and found that there was a trend toward positive outcome and single-level versus multiple-level fusions. Franklin et al. (1994) reported outcome data for all worker's compensation patients receiving lumbar fusion in the state of Washington over a 12-month period beginning August 1986. Results showed that greater work disability outcome was associated with increased number of levels fused. Further, patients receiving instrumentation with fusion had double the risk of reoperation. Other studies, reviewed by Turner et al. (1992), showed no overall advantage for fusion over surgery without fusion in the treatment of herniated discs.

There is good reason to provide minimally destructive procedures. The less invasive surgeries generally allow for shorter hospitalization, more rapid recovery of function, and less long-term impairment. Furthermore, the probability of medical complications, such as deep infections, thrombosis, neural injury, and even death, increase with more extensive surgery. Instrumentation such as rods, plates, and screws, has its own, fairly substantial failure rate of approximately 7% (Turner et al., 1992). For these reasons, destructiveness of surgery is considered a general risk factor. Table 3.3 categorizes the major surgical procedures according to destructiveness.

TABLE 3.3

Relative "Destructiveness" of Invasive Spine Procedures

Minimally Destructive

    Percutaneous discectomy

    Microdiscectomy

    Rhizotomy

    Chymopapain injection

Moderately Destructive

    Foramenotomy

    Open laminectomy/discectomy

    Decompression

Highly Destructive

    Fusion (anterior, posterior, or circumferential)

Note. For all types of procedures, destructiveness escalates as additional levels of the spine are subject to surgery. Surgeries entailing the use of spinal instrumentation are more "destructive" than those that do not.

Nonorganic Signs. Waddell's research on nonorganic signs has had an enormous impact on the assessment of low back pain patients. This procedure is routinely included by many surgeons in their preoperative physical examination. There are a fair number of studies showing that the presence of these nonorganic signs constitutes a major risk factor for poor outcome of spine surgery (e.g., Dzioba & Doxey, 1984). Other studies have shown one of the Waddell signs, nonorganic or "atypical" pain distribution, is associated with poor outcome (Sorenson, 1992). The presence of the nonorganic signs clearly diminishes the probability of good surgical outcome.

Previous Medical Utilization. A number of authors have suggested that patients who are generally prone toward illness may also be less likely to respond to treatment for back pain. Deyo and Diehl (1988), for example, found that positive responses to the question "Do you feel sick all the time?" correlated significantly with poor outcome as assessed by improvement in pain, number of visits to physicians, and compensation seeking. Frymoyer et al. (1983), in an epidemiologic study, found that back pain-related disability was associated with excessive health complaints and illness behaviors. Similarly, Wiltse and Rocchio (1975), found that high scores on the Cornell Medical Index, a questionnaire measuring bodily symptoms and past illnesses, were associated with poor outcome of chemonucleolysis. Ciol, Deyo, Kreuter, and Bigos (1994) found that higher numbers of previous hospitalizations were associated with greater risk of lumbar spine reoperations in a Medicare population. Hoffman et al. (1993), in their review, found that fewer previous hospitalizations were associated with improved discectomy outcome. Thus, patients who have a large number of nonspine-related physical complaints, especially if they received a great deal of treatment for these complaints, should be considered at risk for poor surgical outcome.

Smoking. Smokers have been found, in a number of studies, to be at risk for spine problems. For example, An et al. (1994) found that smokers were much more likely than nonsmokers to have disc herniations. Smoking also has been found to decrease the probability of good surgical outcome. Manniche et al. (1994), for example, found that smokers had a greatly diminished probability of good outcome from discectomy. Similar results have been obtained in patients undergoing repeat fusion by C. Brown, Orme, and Richardson (1986). Recent studies have found that, at least in the case of fusion patients, probability of good surgical outcome may be improved through the use of a bone stimulator, which facilitates the fusion

(K. Lee, 1989, Mooney, 1990). Smoking, however, must still be considered a significant risk factor.

Obesity.   Patients who are greatly overweight should be at higher risk for poor surgical outcome. After all, the effect of obesity should be to place greater physical stress on the structures of the spine. Excessive weight from a large abdomen pulls the lumbar spine forward, placing strain on structures that keep the spine upright—the discs, ligaments, and facets. However, there is no direct evidence of the negative influence of obesity on surgical outcome.

There is, however, research on the general effects of fitness or health status on the outcome of spine treatment, which may be taken as indirect evidence of the negative influence of obesity. Von Korff, Dworkin, and LeResch (1990), examining patients in an HMO, have found that poorer health status is associated with higher, more persistent and more disabling pain complaints. Similarly, Frymoyer and Cats-Baril (1987) found that a low fitness level is associated with greater pain-related disability.

In the absence of any direct empirical outcome-related research, *obesity* (defined as greater than 50% above ideal body weight) is considered to be a moderate predictor of poor outcome.

Summary of Medical Risk Factors

The medical record contains large volumes of information that help the practitioner prepare for the PPS. By combing through this medical information, the patient's medical risk factors for poor outcome should be identifiable. Table 3.4 list the risks factors discussed in the current chapter and gives their overall level of risk.

General Summary and Conclusions

The information and tools provided in this chapter help the behavioral health practitioner to obtain appropriate referrals for PPS, to review the medical records in order to understand patients' medical conditions and planned surgeries, and to make an estimate of each patient's level of medical risk. Thus prepared, the stage is set for an effective and accurate PPS.

One additional point remains, however. It is highly advisable, if at all possible, to make direct contact with the referring physician at some point during the PPS process. Much of what the physician feels about the patient

TABLE 3.4

Medical Risk Factors for Poor Surgical Outcome

Risk Factor	Level of Risk
Chronicity	
Less than 6 months	Low
6–12 months	Moderate
12 months plus	High
Previous Spine Surgeries	
None	Low
One	Moderate
Two or more	High
Destructiveness	
Minimally invasive	Low
Highly invasive	High
Salvage procedures	High
Nonorganic Signs	
Absent	Low
Present	High
Nonspine Medical Utilization	
Minimal	Low
Some complaints and treatment	Moderate
Multiple hospitalizations	High
Smoking	
Absent	Low
Up to 1 pack per day	Moderate
Greater than 1 pack per day	High
Obesity	
None to moderate	Low
Greater than 50% overweight	Moderate

may remain undocumented. In fact, despite finding indications for surgery, the physician may be hoping that the PPS reveals the patient to be a poor surgical candidate. In this way, a problem case may be avoided without the surgeon having to take all the responsibility for the decision not to operate. To the extent that the practitioner can discuss the case with the surgeon prior to the PPS a more complete understanding of the case is obtained.

Chapter 4

Interviewing the Spine Surgery Candidate

The Interview Process

The cornerstone of the PPS is the evaluation interview. It is during this interview that the practitioner has the opportunity to understand the patient's pain problems and how they affect work, family, economics, and lifestyle. The patient's attitude toward the surgery and motivation for improvement in functioning can also be determined. However, interviewing a spine surgery candidate presents unique problems for the behavioral health practitioner. Despite the practitioner's best efforts at helping the surgeon prepare the referral, the patient may not understand why the evaluation is necessary. The patient may or may not know that the outcome of the interview will affect the chances of receiving an operation. Confidentiality issues may also come into play. Thus, initial defensiveness, distrust, and anger often must be overcome.

Further complicating the interview process is the fact that the interview has two basic, and somewhat different goals. First, the interview is the primary source for the identification of many risk factors for poor surgical outcome. Second, psychological treatment planning grows largely out of the results of the interview. These two functions require very different skills and observations. For example, developing rapport is important for planning psychological treatments but relatively unimportant for determining surgical prognosis. Thus, in order to achieve these twin goals of PPS, the practitioner must walk a fine line between empathic understanding and careful information gathering.

In order to deal with these unique problems involving the psychological interview of spine surgery candidates, the suggestions discussed here are offered.

Have a Prepared, Specialized Interview Format.   The PPS interview differs from a traditional mental health evaluation. It requires gathering some very specific information in a short period of time. In many cases, the practitioner will have only one opportunity to meet with the patient, so all factors relevant to risk identification and treatment planning must be gathered during this session. A semistructured interview format is most effective for this purpose. It allows the practitioner to gather the necessary information, but not be tied to a series of mechanical questions. The semistructured interview allows the discussion to cut across a wide range of topics, but always returns to the gathering of specific data. Figure 4.1 represents one possible sample semistructured interview form. Figure 4.2 displays the interview form, with suggestions for specific questions to be asked in order to obtain the necessary information. Specific risk factors assessed during the interview are shown in bold type.

Review Medical Records Prior to the Interview.   As chapter 3 illustrates it is a rather arduous task to review medical information in order to understand the patient's medical condition, planned surgery and identifiable medical risk. However, it is strongly recommended that this review take place prior to the interview. By understanding the basis for the physician's surgical decisions prior to the interview, the practitioner is in a better position to pursue areas of risk. Further, one often finds issues in the medical record which bear discussion with the patient. Such issues might include past non-compliance, overuse of medications, inconsistent diagnoses or test findings. Discussing these problems often can help in determining surgical prognosis.

Explain to the Patient That the PPS is a Routine Procedure.   A psychological evaluation is often the last procedure that a spine surgery candidate expects or wants. The referral for PPS may come as quite a shock. The patient may think that the PPS indicates that the surgeon does not believe the pain is real, or that it is imaginary. The patient may fear that the surgeon thinks he or she is "crazy." In addition, the physician may have told the patient that a surgical problem exists, but that the PPS must be "passed" before surgery can proceed. All of these thoughts, preconceptions, and expectations can set the stage for a stormy or ineffective interview. The patient may be quite defensive, angry, or sullen during the initial phase of the interview. The patient may state outright some opposition to the PPS.

The first key to overcoming resistance to the PPS is to "normalize" the procedure for the patient. It should be explained that the PPS is a routine procedure frequently ordered by the surgeon. The PPS does not indicate that the surgeon is disbelieving of the patient's pain. Rather, PPS is used in most similar cases as a diagnostic test, like any other. It will be used by the surgeon to develop the best overall treatment plan for the patient.

Explain the Purposes and Goals of the PPS. Along with normalizing the evaluation, it is advisable to carefully and tactfully explain to the patient the functions of PPS. It is helpful to tell the patient:

- Spine pain is a condition that can create many problems—emotional, financial, marital, etc. The PPS offers an opportunity to identify and discuss these.
- The interview will help to determine how the patient is likely to affected by the surgery.
- The PPS will help the surgeon to develop the most effective treatment plans.

Begin the Interview With Medically Oriented Information. Because the patient's presenting problem is medical in nature, it is advisable to begin the interview by asking the patient about the injury and current symptoms. This allows one to explore the patient's knowledge about the medical basis of the injury. By empathically listening to the story of the pain and injury, one establishes a level of rapport that will later allow the patient to discuss more emotional and personal issues.

Be Alert for Opportune Moments to Gather Psychological Information. Even the most defensive patient will often provide hints at emotional issues while discussing the medical aspects of the pain. The astute practitioner is alert for these hints and takes the opportunity to explore them. Opportune moments occur when:

- The patient uses "emotional" or "psychological" vocabulary, such as "I feel," "stress," or "pissed off."

Name_____   Date_____
Age____Marital Status_____   Occupation_____
Referring MD_____   Education Level_____
Insurance Type_____   Medical Diag._____
Surgery Planned_____   Height_____Weight_____

Onset   Pain Increasing Conditions:

Pain Site   Pain Decreasing Conditions

Past Procedures   Medications

Blame for injury   Non-spine Medical Problems

Pain Ratings   Least: Now: Worst: Average:

Typical Day: Effect on Family

Sleep   Sex

Appetite   Mood

Concentration & Memory

Stresses   Abuse History

Vocational History & Attitude   Vocational Plans

Current Income Source   Litigation Pending

Coping   Self-Statements

Past Psych Problems   Substance Use History

Recreational Activities   Expectations for outcome

Worst Effect of Injury   Positives in Current Situation

Observations: Recommendations:
Behavior_____ Rating (1 to 5)*
guarding   ____
bracing   ____
grimacing   ____
rubbing   ____
standing   ____
shifting   ____
                                      Actions Taken:
Inconsistency   ____
Bad Rapport   ____
La Belle Ind   ____

1=none to 5=extreme

    FIG. 4.1.   PPS interview form.

Name_____   Date_____
Age____Marital Status_____   Occupation_____
Referring MD_____   **Education Level**_____
Insurance Type_____   Medical Diag._____
Surgery Planned_____   Height_____Weight_____

Onset
  Date of Onset,
  Circumstances
  Remissions & exacerbations
Pain Site
  Primary & secondary pain sites
  Sensations other than pain

Pain Increasing Conditions:
  Activities, environmental conditions
  Psychological states
  Times of day
Pain Decreasing Conditions
  Medications
  Self-regulation techniques
  Positions, modalities

Past Procedures
  Medical & rehab procedures
  Number of previous spine surgeries
  Other procedures
Blame for injury
  Employer
  Self, other, no one

Medications
  Narcotic medications
  Non-narcotic pain medication
  Psychotropics, non pain related meds.
Non Spine Medical Problems
  # of non spine hospitalizations
  Current vs. past medical problems

Pain Ratings   Least: Now: Worst: Average:

Rating Scale: 0 = no pain to 10 = worst pain ever.
Indicate if sensation is not pain but some other sensation

Typical Day:
  Uptime, general activities, naps
  Exercises
  Feelings about average day
Sleep
  Total hours sleep
  Periods of sleeplessness
  Reasons for sleep disturbance
Appetite
  Desire for food last 30 days
  Weight change since injury
  Reasons for weight change

Concentration & Memory
Long vs. Short-term memory
  Pain vs. Non-pain disruptions

Effect on Family
  Marital problems (pre-existing vs. reactive)
  Solicitousness in response to pain
  Spouse's emotional condition
Sex
  How often, how satisfying?
  Adjustments made. Partner's reaction
  sex before injury
Mood
  Depression, anger, irritability
  Frustration & tension
  Emotional state before injury
  Cognitions accompanying emotions

Stresses
  Financial difficulties
  Recent losses or changes
  Does pain vary with stress?
Vocational History & Attitude
  Employment Duration before injury
  Job Satisfaction
  Past employment history
Current Income Source
  Worker's Comp
  Social Security Disability
  Other income sources
Coping
  Activities which reduce or control pain
  Use of self-hypnosis, relaxation
  Hoping and praying?
Past Psych Problems
  Inpatient vs. Outpatient
  Reasons for treatment
  Outcome of treatments
Recreational Activities
  Current enjoyable activities
  Pre injury enjoyable activities
  Does patient have fun?
Worst Effect of Injury
  What is most upsetting about the injury?
  Who does the patient blame for this?

Abuse History
  Physical, mental or sexual abuse
  Current or past?

Vocational Plans
  Return to same employer planned?
  Light duty available?
  Concrete alternative job plans?
Litigation Pending
  Does patient have attorney?
  Actions planned or pending
  Settled cases in regard to injury
Self-Statements
  Has pain changed self-image
  Perceived strengths & weaknesses
  Other self-observations
Substance Use History
  Prescription medication abuse
  Alcohol. Street drugs.
  Smoking?
Expectations for outcome
  Pain Relief: Complete, moderate, none
  Return to work
  Self-responsibility for improvement
Positives in Current Situation
  What is patient happy with?
  How can this not change?

Observations:		Recommendations:
Behavior	Rating (1 to 5)*	
guarding	___	Surgical prognosis
bracing	___	Facultative treatments needed?
grimacing	___	Alternatives to surgery?
rubbing	___	
standing	___	
shifting	___	
		Actions Taken:
Inconsistency	___	
Bad Rapport	___	General notes of referrals, assignments or
La Belle Ind	___	follow-up needed

1=none to 5=extreme

FIG. 4.2.   PPS interview form (with questions identified).

- The client makes "vague references" to intense emotional states, such as, "let's not go into that," "you don't want to know," or "it took me a long time to understand that."
- The client's body language or facial expression indicate intense emotions even though the client does not verbalize these.

Observe Pain Behavior Throughout the Session.   The interview provides an opportunity, not only to gather verbalized information, but also to assess how the patient's functioning and behavior are affected by pain and by interpersonal situations. One should observe how pain behaviors such as shifting weight, rubbing affected areas, and facial pain expressions vary through the course of the session. Particularly, observe differences in pain behavior when the patient's attention is called to this behavior, versus when the patient is distracted.This chapter describes in much greater detail how to systematically observe pain behavior.

Develop Rapport But Don't Let It Determine Your Decision.   All forms of psychological evaluation are more effective to the extent that the practitioner is able to develop a relationship of trust and openness with the patient. Although this is no less true for PPS, the development of rapport is only very small part of identification of risk and determination of prognosis. Patients who are defensive or angry may still be good candidates for surgery. The critical factor is the set of risk factors identified. Rapport becomes important, however, in treatment planning, especially for those patients are poor surgical candidates or alternatives to surgery are undertaken.

Risk Factors and Critical Information

As mentioned earlier, the interview process has two goals. First, during the interview the practitioner can identify many risk factors for poor surgical outcome. Second, information gained during interview allows the practitioner to develop treatment plans—either for facilitating surgical outcome or as alternatives to surgery. This section describes many of the major points covered during the interview in order to achieve the two goals of the PPS interview. It should be noted that some of the factors described in this section have been more extensively researched in predicting the outcome of general spine treatment than in predicting the outcome specifically of spine surgery. Where the preponderance of research relates to nonsurgical outcome studies this will be indicated. Furthermore, some areas, such as emotional states like depression as well as personality factors, are assessed in both the interview and in psychometric tests. These areas are covered in chapter 5.

Financial Factors.   For many years there has been speculation that monetary gain may play a part in the outcome of back pain treatment. For example, as early as 1946, Kennedy stated that many patients have "compensation neurosis"—"a state of mind born out of fear, kept alive by avarice, stimulated by lawyers and cured by verdict." There is some evidence of the influence of pending legal actions on surgical outcome. Haddad (1987), in a very large survey of worker's compensation patients, found that only 9% of patients represented by counsel were working, compared to 77% of those not represented by counsel. Finneson and Cooper (1979) found that both "history of law suits for medicolegal problems" and "secondary gain" predicted negative disc surgery outcome. Manniche et al. (1994) also found that Finneson's criteria predicted poor surgery outcome. Junge et al. (1995), in a study conducted in Switzerland, found that patients who were applying (or considering applying for) for disability pensions had poorer discectomy outcome than did nonapplicants. Thus, pending legal actions and application for disability payments should be considered risk factors.

There is at least one additional financial aspect of spine injuries that predicts poorer outcome. Patients who are injured on the job, are receiving worker's compensation insurance benefits, and are not working seem to fare much more poorly than do working compensation and noncompensation patients. Hudgins (1976), for example, found that patients receiving worker's compensation payments were much less likely to report pain relief and to be working at 1 year postlaminectomy than were noncompensation patients. Similar negative associations of worker's compensation with spine treatment outcome have been found by a number of authors (Davis, 1994; Greenough & Fraser, 1989; Haddad, 1987). Such results have led Frymoyer and Cats-Baril (1987) to state that "compensability" is one of the strongest predictors of excessive disability among back injury patients.

The fact that financial factors may have a negative impact on surgical outcome does not mean that patients frequently malinger (i.e., consciously manufacture symptoms for financial gain). In fact, the large majority of surgical candidates have a pathophysiological condition underlying their pain and disability. Further, surgeons rarely find that patients are malingering. F. Leavitt and Sweet (1986), in a large survey of orthopedic surgeons and neurosurgeons, found that most believe malingering occurs in less than 5% of patients, and it is easily detected. It appears that financial incentives make many of these patients "somatically hypervigilant" (Chapman, 1978;

i.e., acutely aware of and reactive to the pain sensations they experience). Their excessive disability or poor response to treatment, then, is not necessarily manufactured. Rather, it may represent a nonconscious reaction to the combination of pathological condition, personality factors, and environmental conditions.

Vocational Factors.   It is intuitively sensible that the spine surgery candidate's job environment and postoperative vocational plans should make a large difference in recovery. Poorer outcome might be expected in patients who do not like their jobs, do not get along well with their supervisors, or who must return to a job with very heavy physical demands. An even worse situation may occur when the patient's job has been terminated during the course of the injury.

Vocational factors have been found in numerous studies to both predict the occurrence of job-related injuries and the response to treatment for back pain. Bigos et al. (1991), in a major study, followed more than 3,000 aircraft employees for 4 years, examining factors that predicted the occurrence of a job-related back injury. They found that workers reporting the greatest job dissatisfaction, expressed as "I hardly ever enjoy the tasks involved in my job," were 2.5 times more likely to incur a back injury than were their more satisfied colleagues. Such dissatisfaction likely is associated with poorer surgical outcome.

Job demands may also be related to the outcome of spine surgery. Epidemiological research has shown that patients who engage in heavy labor (such as frequent lifting more than 50 pounds) and those whose jobs involve a great deal of travel in cars or trucks are prone to back injuries. In terms of surgical outcome, a number of studies have found that patients having physically demanding jobs are less likely to respond well to surgery (Davis, 1994; Junge et al., 1995). One should, thus, consider a physically demanding job as a predictor of poor outcome.

Substance Use and Abuse.   Many patients with spine pain come to rely on narcotic medication in order to help them function and cope with the pain. Most of these patients take the medication as prescribed and do not develop any problems with drug dependency. However, for a significant minority of spine patients, prescription medication can be a problem. Polatin et al. (1993) found that 19% of spine pain patients entering a work-hardening program had a diagnosable substance abuse problem. Interestingly, almost all of these patients had a history of substance abuse prior to the onset of pain. Other studies (Fishbain, Goldberg, Meagher, Steele, & Rosomoff, 1986) have found a higher rate of substance abuse.

Substance use and abuse is a somewhat underresearched area in spine surgery outcome. Spengler, Freeman, Westbrook, and Miller (1980), reviewing 30 spine surgery failures, found that 25 of the patients "were continually abusing medication and alcohol." Uomoto, Turner, and Herron (1988), in a discriminant analysis of factors predicting laminectomy outcome, found that alcohol abuse was significantly associated with poor results. These results suggest that medication abuse and excessive alcohol use are risk factors to be considered.

Although the identification of alcohol abuse and dependence is relatively straightforward, the definitions of opioid dependence and abuse in spine pain patients are not entirely clear. Physicians vary tremendously in the amount of opioid medication they prescribe, and the extent to which they allow patients to escalate their narcotic use. Some, in fact, suggest the chronic use of opioids for very protracted pain episodes. However, many of the *DSM–IV* (American Psychiatric Association, 1994) diagnostic criteria for substance dependence still can be used for determining whether a spine surgery candidate is dependent on prescription medications. According to the *DSM–IV* criteria, as applied to prescription medication, substance dependence is diagnosable when the patient has at least three of the following behaviors:

- Increasing tolerance of the medication
- Withdrawal symptoms present
- Medications taken in larger amounts and over longer periods than prescribed
- Persistent unsuccessful efforts to reduce medication
- Spending a great deal of time and energy obtaining the medication (e.g., calling multiple doctors to obtain the medication)
- Important work and social activities reduced because of medication use
- Continued medication use even though the patient knows it is causing additional physical or mental problems (e.g., liver or kidney damage)

Marital Interaction. Spine pain affects not only the patient, but also family members and "significant others." There are indications from the literature on chronic pain that the reactions of family members may have a significant influence on patient's motivation and ability to recover from spine injury. Family members may increase the likelihood of extended disability by discouraging the patient from doing any activities, such as exercise, which might provoke some pain increase. They may increase opioid dependence by encouraging the patient to take pain-relieving medications too frequently. Indirect reinforcement of pain behavior may also occur, as when the patient can avoid unwanted sexual advances due to pain. Some studies (e.g., Block et al., 1980a; Lousberg et al., 1992) have demonstrated that when spouses reward pain behaviors, patients are more likely to report high pain levels and display low levels of function in the spouse's presence. Even though this area has not been researched in relation to spine surgery, reinforcement of disability by family members should be considered a risk factor for poor outcome.

There is at least one questionnaire (the West Haven–Yale Pain Inventory; Kerns, Turk, & Rudy, 1985), containing a section that has been widely used to assess spousal reinforcement of pain behavior. In our laboratory we assess spouse response to pain behavior by asking the patient a standardized series of questions. The patient is asked to rate the likelihood of various spousal responses to pain on a scale of 0 (*no likelihood*) to 10 (*absolute certainty*). The patient's perception of spouse response to pain behavior is calculated from answers to the following nine items:

> When you are in extreme pain, how likely is your spouse to : (a) express sympathy; (b) bring you medication; (c) give you a massage; (d) ignore you; (e) tell you not to exert yourself; (f) express anger at you; (g) bring you presents; (h) express frustration with you; (I) take over your jobs and duties?

A spouse-response score (SRS) is calculated by summing the values for items a, b, c, e, g, and i (those items indicating reinforcement for pain behavior) and subtracting the combined values of items d, f, and h (those items indicating no reinforcement or negative sanctions for pain behavior). This formula yields scores that range from -30 to +60. Our research has found that the patient perceives a high level of spousal reinforcement if the total SRS score is above 20 (Block et al., 1980a).

Family members may also have a negative effect on the outcome of treatment for a very different reason. A number of studies have shown that spouses, especially wives, of back pain patients may be depressed and very dissatisfied with their marriages (Romano, Turner, & Clancy, 1989; L. Schwartz, Slater, Birchler, & Atkinson, 1991). Dissatisfied spouses have been found to have more negative outcome expectations for patients (Block, Boyer, & Silbert, 1985), and to attribute the patient's pain to psychological problems (Block & Boyer, 1984). Sexual difficulties are also common (Maruta & Osborne, 1976). Thus, marital dissatisfaction may be associated with poor treatment outcome. Giving the Locke–Wallace (1959) inventory of marital satisfaction to both the patient and the spouse is a quick way to assess this important factor.

Abuse.   Negative interaction with family members may go well beyond dissatisfaction. There is evidence that many spine surgery candidates have a history of physical or sexual abuse, either as an adult or in childhood. Haber and Roos (1985), found that 53% of women evaluated at a multidisciplinary pain center were physically or sexually abused and that for 90% of victims the abuse occurred during adulthood. The abused women were more likely to have "spontaneously arising pain" and to have significantly more medical problems in their history. Sexual and physical abuse have also been found to be associated with a number of other chronic pain syndromes (see chapter 8) such as chronic pelvic pain (Reiter, 1990) and chronic gastrointestinal pain (Drossman et al., 1990).

Physical and sexual abuse may also influence the treatment of spine pain. In a recent fascinating retrospective study, Schofferman et al. (1992) investigated the existence of five types of childhood psychological trauma in spine surgery patients. The traumatic events included physical abuse, sexual abuse, parental substance abuse, abandonment, and emotional abuse. Of the patients who reported three or more of these traumatic events, 85% had unsuccessful surgical outcome, versus a 5% failure rate among patients reporting none of these traumatic events. Therefore, sexual and physical abuse, either past or present, is considered a surgical risk factor.

Past Psychological Treatment.   Spine pain patients often have a history of significant psychological difficulties. Kinney, Gatchel, Polatin, Fogarty, and Mayer (1993), for example, assessed 90 chronic and low back pain patients using the *DSM–III–R* Structured Clinical Interview (SCID). All of the chronic patients had diagnosable psychological problems compared to 61% of the acute pain sufferers. Although lower incidence rates of diagnosable disorders in chronic low back pain patients have been found in other studies (e.g., Coste, Paolaggi, & Spira, 1992b), it is clear that psychological problems are very common among spine pain patients.

There currently exists a controversy about whether psychological disturbance results from (Gamsa, 1992) or precedes back pain (Polatin et al., 1993). However, a number of authors have found or suggested that patients with preexisting psychological disturbance recover more poorly from back injuries (Keel, 1984; Polatin et al., 1993). This certainly accords well with a diathesis–stress model of psychopathology. According to such a model, individuals who develop some psychological weakness can maintain emotional stability during periods of low stress, but may decompensate under periods of high stress. As spine pain is, by its nature, a highly stressful event, patients with preexisting psychological disturbance may not be able to maintain emotional stability especially under the strain of surgery. There is some limited direct evidence of the role of preexisting psychological disturbance in influencing surgical outcome. In the Manniche et al. (1994) study, the Finneson score (which includes "poor psychological background") was a very strong predictor of poor surgical outcome. Thus, prior psychological disturbance, especially if it resulted in inpatient treatment, can be considered a risk factor for poor surgical outcome.

Interview Risk Factor Summary

The relative risk for the factors identified during the interview are displayed in Table 4.1. These risk factors will be combined with other psychological factors to be identified through the interview and observation (chapter 5), to determine overall level of psychological risk.

TABLE 4.1
Risk Factors for Poor Surgical Outcome Identified in the PPS Interview

Risk Factor	Risk Level
Pending legal actions related to injury	High risk
Worker's compensation	High risk
Job dissatisfaction	
moderate	Moderate risk
extreme	High risk
Heavy job demands (frequent lifting > 50 lb)	High risk
Substance Abuse	
preinjury	Moderate risk
current	High risk
Reinforcement of disability by family members	Moderate to high risk
Marital dissatisfaction	Moderate risk
Physical or sexual abuse	
preinjury	Moderate risk
current	High risk
Preinjury psych problems	
outpatient treatment	Moderate risk
inpatient treatment	High risk

Interview Topics Relevant to Treatment Planning

In addition to identifying risk factors, through the interview the practitioner comes to learn many aspects of the patient's personality, emotional state, and social situation. The interview provides the opportunity for understanding the patient's perspective on his or her injury, motivation for improvement, and how the injury fits into the patient's overall situation. As a result, the practitioner should be able to develop suggestions for individualizing treatment plans so as to improve surgical outcome. In addition, the interview should allow the practitioner to identify problem areas that would respond to psychotherapy or other mental health treatments.

Strengths and Weaknesses. Spine pain and spine surgery tax the resources of even the most emotionally stable individuals. The astute practitioner can learn a great about the patient's abilities to handle such difficulties by exploring the patient's responses to other major medical problems and traumatic situations. Questions that identify relevant strengths and weaknesses can focus on:

- Adaptive or maladaptive emotional responses to past medical problems and difficult times
- Stress management techniques the patient has developed or learned
- Family and social support during difficult times
- Mistakes made in dealing with stress, such as giving up or catastrophizing
- Lessons learned from dealing with these difficulties

Motivation for Psychological Intervention. If a psychological treatment is proposed to either facilitate surgical outcome or as an alternative to surgery, it is critical that the patient be motivated for such an approach. Motivation is a complex issue and its assessment requires careful consideration, not only of the patient, but of the context in which the psychological evaluation occurs. A patient who feels threatened or poorly understood may express defensive answers to questions, even while truly feeling strongly motivated for psychological intervention. Drawing largely on the writing of Sifneos (1987), the following suggestions are offered for assessing motivation for psychological intervention among spine pain patients. The practitioner should examine:

- Willingness to participate and active involvement in evaluation
- Honesty in reporting symptoms (by observing inconsistencies in reporting, manipulation, and nonverbal behavior)
- Recognition of influence of emotional states on pain perception
- Curiosity about insights and information discussed by practitioner
- Positive changes that the patient feels will result from recovery
- Realistic outcome expectations, recognizing there will still be some limits and perhaps postoperative pain
- Has patient sought counseling before the injury to deal with problems?

Self-Responsibility for Improvement.   The spine surgery candidate is trusting his or her future to the surgeon. It is expected that surgery will result in reduction in pain and improvement in functioning. However, the recovery process only begins with the spine surgery. In order to maximize improvements, the patient must play a major role, participating in aggressive physical conditioning programs, tolerating pain with minimal use of narcotics, and making adjustments in life. The practitioner can use the interview to assess the patient's enthusiasm for participating in his or her own treatment, by examining some of the following points:

- Willingness to make sacrifices, such as reducing medications, losing weight, or stopping smoking prior to surgery, or adjusting schedules to fit those of provider
- Desire to learn information about the injury, surgery, and rehabilitation techniques
- Willingness to learn pain control techniques, such as self-hypnosis or biofeedback. Explore pain control techniques the patient has spontaneously developed
- Commitment to a postoperative treatment plan, involving their active participation

Behavioral Observations

The practitioner gains information during the interview not only through the patient's responses to questions, but also by observing the patient's behavior. Behavioral observation is always a major part of the behavioral health practitioner's training. Behaviors relevant to mental status, such as grooming, posture, eye contact (cf. Othmer & Othmer, 1991) or other mental status behavior) are also critical in the PPS. Additionally, rapport (therapist's impression of the patient's general emotional responsiveness) is important—particularly for treatment planning. However, there are some behavioral observations that are specific to PPS for which the behavioral health practitioner receives little or no training.

Spending 1 to 2 hours with a spine pain patient allows the practitioner to observe many "pain behaviors." Such overt manifestations of the patient's pain experience may vary throughout the course of the session, perhaps corroborating or contradicting information the patient gives about pain-provoking situations. One may also be able to observe the emotional impact of the injury and pain. All of these observations can be important in both reaching a surgical prognosis and in treatment planning.

Direct Observation of Pain Behaviors. The patient who is experiencing back pain is frequently unable to sit, stand, or walk comfortably. This discomfort is most often apparent. It can be observed as "pain behaviors," such as distorted gait; abnormal seated position; facial pain expressions such as grimacing; and the like. Keefe and Block (1982) developed a method for quantifying such pain behaviors through direct behavioral observation. In this procedure, the patient is videotaped while engaging in a series of movements, including walking, sitting down, standing, and so on. Five types of pain behaviors are defined:

- Guarding—stiff, interrupted movement
- Bracing—using a limb to abnormally support weight
- Rubbing—touching the affected area
- Grimacing—a facial expression of pain
- Sighing—exaggerated exhalation of breath

Trained observers rated the videotapes for the presence of these behaviors. In this initial study, the behavioral observation techniques were found to be very reliable across observers. Furthermore, patient's pain ratings on a scale of 0 to 10 were found to be highly correlated with overall pain behaviors ($r = .67$), and even more closely correlated with guarding ($r = .81$). The Keefe and Block (1982) procedures for observing pain behavior have received a number of replications and extensions (Baumstark et al., 1993; Buckelew et al., 1994; McDaniel et al., 1986).

Practitioners performing the PPS are not able to perform the careful quantification of pain behaviors entailed in the Keefe and Block procedure. However, the practitioner's observation of pain behaviors can give a number of important clues to the patient's pain perception and response to treatment. The critical issue for the practitioner centers around consistency. That is, how consistent are the patient's pain behaviors with his or her own reports of pain and pain-provoking events?

Keeping in mind the pain behavior categories previously defined, the practitioner should observe pain behaviors in a number of ways. First, compare pain behaviors with reported pain levels to determine consistency. The pain experience may be suspect in patients who report a high level of subjective pain but show no obvious indications. Second, observe behavior during pain-provoking conditions such as movement, lengthy time in a seated position, and so on. This may entail asking the patient to make certain movements during the session, such as getting up out of a seated position, reclining, or walking. Such pain-provoking conditions may give clues to situations that may make the patient focus on pain or situations where pain management techniques should be applied.

A final suggestion concerning behavioral observation is to observe pain behaviors under different conditions of observation. As noted earlier, Waddell (1987) found that nonorganic signs of low back pain, such as difficulty with straight leg raising, occurred with greater intensity when the patient was aware that the behavior was being observed than with distraction (chapter 2). Patients may also show varying amounts of pain behavior with observational conditions. In order to assess this, the practitioner should observe pain behaviors at every opportunity—while the patient is in the waiting room, walking to the session, taking psychological testing, and so on. At least once during the interview, if the patient displays any pain behavior, the practitioner should point this out and observe any behavioral changes. Consistency in pain behavior under different observational conditions indicates that the patient's subjective pain experience and its objectively observable consequences are well correlated.

La Belle Indifference.   A number of patients report the experience of a high level of pain accompanied by greatly decreased functioning, but appear emotionally indifferent to these problems. In discussing their pain, and even while reporting pain, or perhaps displaying pain behaviors, these patients appear blasé, or sometimes even happy and positive. Such patients display an air of "somatization without distress"—heightened pain sensitivity with minimal emotional response.

Somatization without distress or *la belle indifference* is another form of inconsistency (i.e., inconsistent behavior and affect). This pattern is frequently identified from psychological test results, as is seen in chapter 5. However, the practitioner who can observe this inconsistent pattern is in a better position to determine the role that psychological intervention may play in the patient's overall treatment plan. Clearly, with such patients, an appeal to deal with the emotional consequences of pain is likely to fall on deaf ears.

Behaviors Affected by Substance Use.   Spine pain patients take narcotic medications in order to control their pain level. As noted previously, however, use of these medications can develop into substance abuse or dependence. Patient reports about medication use and its effects are not always nor completely reliable. Therefore, one way to determine whether such problems exist is to observe the patient's pain behaviors, as well as medication-dependent behaviors, during the interview. First, observe signs of opioid intoxication, including somnolence, slurred speech, and retarded thought processes (see *DSM–IV* for additional signs). Second, consider the effects of opioids on pain behavior. Is the medication effective in helping the patient be functional or does the patient still display high levels of pain behavior despite medication intake? For some patients, medications serve to mask the pain so they can continue to function at a high level, whereas others are made more dysfunctional by medication. Finally, be alert to medication-seeking behavior. It is frequently the case that, if the patient asks the behavioral health practitioner to assist in obtaining new narcotic prescriptions, then the patient may have been overusing medications. As substance abuse is a predictor of poor surgical outcome, medication-seeking behavior during the interview may be a critical negative factor to the decision on surgical prognosis and to treatment planning.

Summary

The evaluation interview is the most critical component of PPS. The interview allows the practitioner, through observation and questioning the patient, to evaluate many risk factors for poor surgical outcome. Additionally, information gained during the interview assist in the development of treatment plans to facilitate surgical outcome, as well as identifying treatment alternatives to surgery. Observation of behavior during the PPS enhances the practitioners decision-making ability. The interview, however, is not the only source of critical psychological information. Psychological testing allows the practitioner to make a more complete, accurate, and objective assessment of the patient. By combining these sources of information, the behavioral health practitioner is able to offer the surgeon an ideal approach for maximizing improvements while minimizing the use of ineffective treatment approaches.

Chapter 5

Psychometric Testing of Spine Surgery Candidates: Personality and Cognition

Many of the symptoms suffered by the spine surgery candidate are difficult to assess objectively. Pain is a subjective sensation, one that cannot be directly or concretely measured. Sleep disturbance cannot be observed unless the patient is brought into a sleep laboratory. Depression is an emotional experience that depends, to a large extent, on highly personal responses to stress. The patient may have difficulty recognizing, much less articulating, a large part of this and other affective states. Thus, much of the experience of the spine pain patient lies beyond the realm of direct assessment.

The subjective nature of symptoms suffered by the spine surgery candidate creates the need for some concrete, valid measures of psychological functioning. Fortunately, such measures are available in the form of psychometric testing. Psychometric testing, as used with spine surgery candidates, primarily involves the use of paper-and-pencil questionnaires. The questionnaires, as described in this practice guide, have been developed through rigorous, scientifically accepted, test-development process. Most of these questionnaires have been given to thousands, or in some cases millions of subjects, so the results are quite reliable and reproducible. Psychometric testing, at its best, can offer results that are objective, standardized, and free from the influence of the patient's behavioral presentation.

Psychometric testing, within the context of PPS, serves three major functions. First, testing has a descriptive purpose. In a relatively short period of time it can offer an objective "snapshot" of the patient, revealing many aspects of the patient's personality and current emotional state. It is this descriptive function that also probes the patient's thought processes, articulating distorted, irrational, or "maladaptive" perceptions, as well psychotic thinking. Further, testing can describe environmental influences on the patient, such as martial and job satisfaction, stress level, and sources of secondary gain. In short, psychometric testing can be an effective and scientifically validated means to characterize the PPS patient's personality, behavior, and cognition.

A second important function of psychometric testing is that it can be used to predict treatment outcome and adjust treatment plans. Testing may reveal which types of treatments offer the best opportunities for improvements, and which treatments may offer little hope of success. It may reveal inner strengths and coping skills that can be drawn on to overcome problems, as well as weaknesses that must be taken into account. It may reveal potential sources of resistance, as well as areas that may improve compliance. In other words, psychometric testing can offer many suggestions to guide and individualize treatment.

The final major reason for including psychometric testing within the PPS is that it serves as a check on the practitioner's perceptions of the patient. For example, not infrequently a patient may report minimal feelings of depression, but psychometric testing may reveal a much higher level of clinical depression symptomatology. On the other hand, some patients who present with extreme complaints of psychological distress may have psychological test results revealing that they tend to exaggerate symptoms, perhaps as a "cry for help." Thus, psychometric testing may either validate or challenge the practitioner's perceptions of the patient.

Unfortunately, psychometric testing is not always a part of the behavioral health practitioner's training. In the absence of such instruction, it is difficult to understand many of the critical features that underlie the construction and validation of the psychometric test being used. It may, therefore, be difficult to know the limitations of the testing, as well as the strength of possible testing-based conclusions. Furthermore, many tests, such as the MMPI, the Millon Behavioral Health Inventory (MBHI), and the SCL-90, give results in terms of multiple scales. Thorough training in these tests may be necessary to understand and interpret the complex patterns of scale elevations that can be obtained.

A huge literature exists on psychometric testing of back pain patients. This chapter provides an overview of this literature, particularly as it applies to prediction of outcome and individualization of treatment in spine surgery candidates. It is not the purpose of this chapter to provide an exhaustive and critical review of such testing. Further, an understanding of test construction and validation is beyond the scope of this text (see Anastasi, 1994, for basic information on psychometrics). Rather, it is hoped that this chapter provides the reader with sufficient information to use psychometric testing as one component of PPS, in order to develop scientifically sound and clinically astute patient descriptions, treatment plans, and predictions of surgical outcome.

Personality Testing

The experience of back pain affects each patient in a unique and highly personal way. Each patient brings to bear a variety of perceptions, strengths and weaknesses, habits, and traits in coping with pain and its effects. These differences are, to some extent, a product of differences in "personality."

Personality has been defined as "deeply ingrained patterns of behaviors, which include the way one relates to, perceives and thinks about the environment and oneself" (American Psychiatric Association, 1987, p. 1). Personality testing aims to document or describe these patterns, through the patient's responses to a series of questions. Some tests, such as the MMPI-2, describe personality in terms of characteristics associated with various psychological disorders, such as hysteria, depression and obsessive–compulsive disorder. Others, such as the 16 PF (Cattell, Eber, & Tatsuoka, 1970), describe personality in terms of the patient's scores on "normal" traits, such as extroversion, warmth, or suspiciousness. Whichever is the case, personality tests can provide a wealth of important descriptive information.

The MMPI and MMPI-2. The MMPI (and its more recent version, the MMPI-2) is the psychometric test that has been most widely used in the assessment of back pain patients generally, as well as in the prediction of spine surgery outcome. For this reason, a more detailed overview of information about the MMPI is in order. In discussing the MMPI, I also include possible explanations for the results obtained in published research reports.

Each patient's results on the MMPI are given as a series of scores or "elevations" on 3 "validity" scales and 10 "clinical" scales, as well as supplemental scales. Generally, the practitioner, as well as the research literature, focuses on excessively high scales scores, that is, those scores at least 1.5 standard deviations above the mean (i.e., T score > 65). The 3 validity scales, L, F, and K, assess test-taking attitude, such as exaggeration or denial of emotional difficulties, as well as degree of psychopathology. The 10 clinical scales are summarized in Table 5.1.

There have been a huge number of studies on the use of the MMPI with chronic pain patients (for a review see Keller & Butcher, 1992). However, there have been far fewer studies assessing the relationship of elevations on MMPI scales to the outcome of spine surgery. These studies examining spine surgery outcome are summarized in Table 5.2.

Although it is not apparent in Table 5.2, much of the research is retrospective in nature. That is, the studies were often conducted by chart review (e.g., Long, 1981). Furthermore, the types of outcome measures used in these studies vary greatly. In some studies (e.g., Long, 1981; Wiltse & Rocchio, 1975), outcome is assessed by the surgeon's global estimates of overall success or failure. Many studies use some variant of the Stauffer and Coventry (1972) criteria (see chapter 1 of this practice guide). These criteria focus on four types of outcome: medication use, pain relief, work

TABLE 5.1

MMPI: General Overview of High Scores on Clinical Scales

Scale	Description
1	Hs (hypochondriasis): concern about health and somatic functioning
2	D (depression): low morale
3	Hy (hysteria): tendencies toward somatic complaints or denial of emotional distress
4	Pd (antisocial): reflects impulsivity
5	Mf (masculinity–femininity):identification with stereotyped masculine or feminine role
6	Pa (paranoia): elevation suggests suspiciousness and/or paranoid characteristics; the absence of elevation does not preclude the existence of these characteristics
7	Pt (psychasthenia): anxiety
8	Sc (schizophrenia): disorganized thinking
9	Ma (hypomania): reflects expansiveness
10	Si (social introversion): discomfort in interpersonal relations

TABLE 5.2

MMPI Predictors of Poor Surgical Outcome or Surgical Failure

Author(s)	Surgery Type	Follow-Up Interval	MMPI Predictors
Cashion & Lynch (1979)	laminectomy	12 mos	**F, -K, Hs, D**
Doxey et al. (1988)	various	12 mos	**HS**, Ma, Pt
Dvorak et al. (1988)	unclear	4–17 yrs	**Hy, Hs, D, Pt,** Sc, Pa, Pd
Herron et al. (1992)	laminectomy	12–50 mos	**Hs,** Hy, D, Pd, F, Pt
Kuperman, Osmon, Golden, & Blume (1979)	discectomy	12 mos	Hs, Hy, D; esp. **Hs+Hy+D**
Long (1981)	various	6–18 mos	**Hy,** Hs, D, Pd
Pheasant et al. (1979)	various	6–12 mos	**Hs, Hy,** D
Riley et al. (1995)[a]	fusion	6 mos+	**Hs–Hy, Pathological cluster including Hs, D, HY, Pa, Pt, Sc**
Smith & Duerksen (1979)	various	unclear	**Hs, Hy,** D
Sorenson & Mors (1988)	discectomy	6–24 mos	**Hy, Hs, D, Sc, Ma,** Pd, Pa, Pt
Spengler et al. (1990)	discectomy	> 1 yr	**Hs, Hy, Pd, Sc**
Turner et al. (1986)	laminectomy	1 yr	**Hs,** Hy
Wiltse & Rocchio (1975)	chemonucleolysis	1 yr	**Hs + Hy**

Note. Strongest predictors shown in bold type
[a]Examined MMPI profiles clusters in relationship to outcome (see text)

status, and pain-related restrictions in nonwork activity. In most studies, outcome is assessed by surgeon or practitioner ratings, rather than patient self-reports. Doxey, Dzioba, and Mitson (1988), however, used both orthopedic ratings of outcome and patient opinion of outcome.

The results displayed in Table 5.2 reveal that, despite all the variations in research quality and protocols, a number of consistent findings have been obtained. First, scales *Hy* and *Hs* are found, in almost all studies to be associated with poor surgical outcome. Elevated *D* scores also frequently accompany failure of spine surgery. Found less frequently are scales *Pd, Sc,* and *Pt* elevations. These various individual scale elevations and multiple scale configurations have a number of possible explanations and implications for prognosis.

Discussion of MMPI Findings

Hs and Hy Elevations.   The most consistent MMPI elevations associated with poor surgical outcome are on scale *Hs* and *Hy.* This finding is not surprising because both of these scales were designed to identify patients with a propensity for excessive physical complaints (Graham, 1990). Further, it is well established that elevations on *Hs* and *Hy* are associated with excessive pain complaints and poor treatment outcome in a number of physical disorders, including gastrointestinal disorder (Whitehead, 1993) and pelvic pain (Rosenthal, Ling, Rosenthal, & McNeeley, 1984; see chapter 8). In the conservative treatment of chronic back pain high *Hs* and *Hy* bode poorly for outcome (Kleinke & Spangler, 1988a).

There are a number of possible explanations for the poor results obtained by patients having elevated *Hs* and *Hy* scores. The original explanantion (Engle, 1959), based on a psychoanalytic perspective, used the term *conversion V* to describe elevations on these two scales. According to such a psychoanalytic formulation, unconscious anxiety, arising from childhood experiences, is converted to into physical complaints (see chapter 2). Thus, the patient avoids having to experience the emotional distress. However, as noted by Gamsa (1994) and others (Main & Spanswick, 1995), there is little evidence to support a pure psychoanalytic interpretation of the conversion V profile.

There are, however, at least two alternative, nonexclusive explanations for the poor outcome obtained by patients have such elevations. First, it may be that patients with *Hs* and/or *Hy* elevations are simply *oversensitive* to pain. That is, they have a subjective perception of great pain with minimal tissue damage. Second, following from the *operant conditioning* perspective expressed by Fordyce, patients with these MMPI elevations may be complaining of high pain levels because they have received reinforcement or reward for such complaints. There is evidence to support both such explanations.

The concept of oversensitivity to pain and physical symptoms draws support from studies that examine the patient's response to an induced pain stimulus. Research by Schmidt (1987; Schmidt & Brands, 1986) subjected chronic low back pain patients to a cold pressor test (i.e., immersion of forearm into an ice water bath). Results showed that the patients both reported higher pain levels and tolerated the ice water for a shorter period of time than did a control, nonpatient group.

Even stronger support for an oversensitivity explanation is seen in research conducted at our laboratory (Block et al., 1996). This study examined patients' pain reports during discography (see chapter 3). Discograms are often performed on surgical candidates having suspected disc disruption or degeneration. In discography, the disc nucleus is injected with radiographic contrast material. A postdiscogram CT scan permits visualization of the disc, in order to determine whether is it damaged. If the disc is disrupted, the injection frequently provokes the patient's normally ocurring pain, whereas injection of a nondisrupted disc is not pain provocative. In our study, the MMPI was given to a series of patients prior to undergoing three lumbar discograms. We found that almost half of the patients reported pain reproduction on injection of at least one normal-appearing disc. That is, for these patients, pain perception was not concordant with the CT disc image. Patients who reported such nonconcordant pain were much more likely to have elevated scores on MMPI scales *Hs* and *Hy* than were patients whose pain reports were consistent with CT images. Thus, it appears patients with elevated *Hs* and *Hy* scales (scores above 70 on the MMPI-2), show evidence of excessive pain sensitivity.

Support for an operant explanation of the association of *Hs* and *Hy* with poor outcome is also seen. Bigos et al.(1991), as noted earlier, showedhat individuals with elevated *Hy* scores are much more likely to report job-related injuries than are those without such elevations. Dvorak, Valach, Fuhrimann, and Heim (1988), examining follow-up results on spine surgery patients, found that those patients who were retired on a pension had a very high likelihood of elevated *Hs* and *Hy* scores. Several studies have shown that have shown that pain reports (Block et al., 1980a) and pain behaviors (Lousberg et al., 1994) can be increased in operant fashion by the actions of the spouse in response to pain behavior. Taken together, all these studies support an operant explanation (see chapter 2).

There is, likely, truth in both the operant and oversensitivity explanations for the poor results obtained by patients with elevated *Hs* and *Hy* scores. It seems likely that in many cases, the patient's focus on and distress at the pain experience results in reinforcing responses by others. The legal system provides financial incentives for pain experience. The spouse may frequently ask the patient about pain, as much to relieve his or her own distress as to express support for the patient. Thus, it seems likely environmental reinforcers and pain sensation interact with each other.

D Scale Elevations.   As seen in Table 5.2, a number of studies have found D scale elevations to be associated with poor surgical outcome, although this finding is far from universal. It is, perhaps, not surprising that depression is a predictor of poor results. Depressed individuals have been found to have a low threshold for induced pain (Merskey, 1965). They have been found to be likely to focus on and remember negative, rather than positive events (Seligman, 1975). In chronic pain patients, depression has been found to be associated with underreporting of improvements from rehabilitation (Kremer et al., 1983). In general, depressed individuals experience decreased motivation, energy and low self-esteem sufficient to diminish the likelihood of improvement.

The elevated D scores seen in spine surgery candidates may have many causes. An examination of the basis for these scores may be crucial for determining the impact of D elevations on surgical outcome. First, many of the vegetative symptoms of depression, such as sleep disturbance, weight change, decreased motivation, and decreased sexual desire may result more from the pain or illness than from clinical depression (Cavanaugh, Clark, & Gibbons, 1983). Furthermore, the pain creates conditions that have been found to produce clinical depression, such as a decrease in enjoyable activities and a loss of control. Perhaps this is the reason that clinical depression is found in up to 85% of chronic pain patients (Lindsay & Wyckoff, 1981). If the patient's depressive symptoms are a reaction to the pain and dysfunction, then treatment of the pain source should lead to a concomitant improvement in these symptoms. For many such patients with reactive depression, antidepressant medication might be also be considered prior to surgery.

On the other hand, many patients have chronic or recurrent depression (dysthymia) that predates the spine injury. Polatin et al. (1993) reported that 39% of chronic low back pain patients they evaluated displayed symptoms of preexisting depressive symptoms. Such patients with protracted, preinjury depressive symptoms would seem more likely to retain the symptoms of depression after surgery. Thus, they may continue to display low levels of function and motivation, sleep disturbance, and other vegetative signs. Therefore, those patients with elevated D scores (above T score of 70), especially when depression predates the injury, are at risk for poor outcome.

Pd Elevations.   Elevations on scale *Pd* have been associated with poor surgical outcome in five studies (Dvorak et al., 1988; Herron, Turner, Ersek, & Weiner, 1992; Long, 1981; Sorenson & Mors, 1988; Spengler et al., 1990). This scale was originally designed to identify patients with an amoral or antisocial personality type. However, more recently two major themes have emerged from research on scale *Pd*. First, these patients tend to be rebellious toward authority figures. Second, they tend to be hostile and aggressive (Graham, 1990).

The characteristics of rebelliousness and anger would not seem to bode well for treatment outcome. Unfortunately, Turk and Fernandez (1995), in a review article, found anger to be quite common among chronic pain patients. Furthermore, DeGood and Kiernan (1996), found that anger about the cause of the injury can affect the outcome of treatment. In this study, chronic pain patients who placed blame for the injury on the employer, tended to have a high level of mood disturbance and poor treatment response.

It is understandable that *Pd* elevations may be associated with poor surgical outcome. Patients who are angry, rebellious toward authority figures such as physicians, and tend to blame others for their problems, may be less likely to establish an alliance with health care providers (Fernandez & Turk, 1995) and thus, are unlikely to comply with treatment recommendations. They may get into confrontations with staff members. They may experience little remorse at such problematic behaviors. Thus, *Pd* elevations (*T* score > 70) are considered predictors of poor outcome.

Other Single-Scale Elevations.   A number of other MMPI scales have received limited support as predictors of poor surgical results. The most strongly supported of these scales is *Pt* (Doxey et al., 1988; Dvorak et al., 1988; Herron et al., 1992; Sorenson & Mors, 1988). *Pt* was originally designed to identify symptoms that are similar to obsessive–compulsive disorder: excessive doubts, compulsions, obsessions, and unreasonable fears. It is also a good index of psychological turmoil (Graham, 1990).

Compulsive traits are quite common among patients with spine pain. Fishbain et al. (1986) found that nearly 25% of chronic pain patients had compulsive personality types and almost 7% had obsessive–compulsive personality disorders. According to the *DSM–IV* (American Psychiatric Association, 1994), patients with such disorders tend to be stubborn, rigid, and inflexible. They also tend to be self-critical. In spine pain patients, who often have to adapt to an altered lifestyle, such traits may present major difficulties.

No other single MMPI scale elevations have sufficient empirical support to be considered as scientifically valid predictors of poor surgical outcome. However, some trends on the MMPI appear to be emerging in the research literature. First, in many studies seen in Table 5.2, poor responders show greater elevations on many MMPI scales than do nonresponders, although these differences do not obtain significance. However, it seems likely that, with a sufficient number of subjects, other scales, such as *Sc* and *Ma,* may differentiate good from poor responders.

Multiple Scale Elevations.   In the assessment of chronic pain patients, MMPI research has moved from an examination of single-scale elevations to an analysis of consistent MMPI profiles patterns (see Bradley, Prokop, Gentry, Van der Heide, & Prieto, 1981). Using cluster analysis techniques applied to MMPI-2 responses of chronic pain patients, Keller and Butcher (1991) identified three consistent male profiles and three consistent female profiles. These MMPI profiles tend to have three basic patterns: a cluster of elevations on scales *Hs, D,* and *Hy;* a pattern with elevations on many scales; and a pattern wherein all scales are within normal limits.

Only one study has applied cluster analysis techniques to the MMPI-2 profiles of surgical candidates (Riley, Robinson, Geisser, Wittmer, & Smith, 1995). This study identified four profile types in 201 patients, 71 of whom underwent spinal fusion (Fig. 5.1). Outcome was assessed at 6 months after surgery. Results showed that the "V-type" and "depressed-pathological" groups reported greater dissatisfaction with the procedure than did the other two groups. Using the Stauffer and Coventry (1972) criteria (see chapter 3), surgical outcome was found to be predicted by profile type. The "within-normal-limits" group showed significantly greater improvement than did the "V-type" group, but were no different than the "depressed-pathological" nor the "triad" group. Unfortunately, only 4 patients displayed depressed-pathological profiles, so the results in this group are difficult to interpret.

The Riley et al. (1995) results point to some intriguing conclusions. It appears that patient with a "V–type pattern" of *Hs* and *Hy* elevations may fare more poorly than those with a "triad" pattern of *Hs, Hy,* and *D* elevations. Patients with the multiple scale elevations termed *depressed-pathological* may also not obtain good outcomes. Unfortunately, although these implications of the Riley et al. (1995) study provide important directions for future research, there exists insufficient scientific evidence to base PPS predictions on multiple scale elevations.

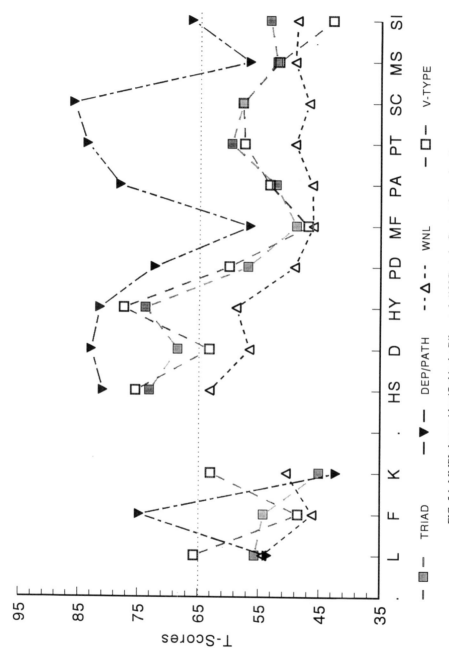

FIG. 5.1. MMPI clusters identified in the Riley et al. (1995) study. See text for explanation (from Riley et al., 1995. Reprinted by permission of Lippincott-Raven Publishers).

Other Personality Tests

Millon Behavioral Health Inventory. Unlike the MMPI, which was developed to assess personality characteristics associated with mental disorders, the ostensible purpose of MBHI is to provide information describing the patient's personality and style as these relate to medical treatment. The MBHI provides normative information on the patient's general interactions with health care personnel. Further, it assesses current stressful events and the patient's tendency to react to stress with increases in physical symptoms. Finally, it purports to indicate the patient's probable response to medical treatment in general, and specifically to treatments designed to reduce pain. For these reasons, the MBHI is of potential value in screening surgical candidates.

There has been relatively little work on the utility of MBHI as an outcome predictor in either chronic pain or in spine surgery. Barnes, Smith, Gatchel, and Mayer (1989) found that three MBHI scales, *Cooperative, Forceful,* and *Premorbid Pessimism,* predicted premature drop out from a functional restoration program. However, Gatchel, Mayer, Capra, Barnett, and Diamond (1986) did not find that any MBHI scales differentially predicted outcome of such a program.

In the area of spine surgery there have been two studies on the MBHI. Orme, Brown, and Richardson (1985) compared the outcome of unspecified types of spine surgery in patients who had at least one highly elevated MBHI scale (score greater than 75), versus patients with no highly elevated scores. In a 2-year follow-up, Orme et al. found that this MBHI distinction correctly classified 76% of surgical successes and 88% of surgical failures. A second study (Herron et al., 1992), however, provides little support for the use of the MBHI as an outcome predictor. In this study, patients undergoing lumbar laminectomy were given both the MMPI and the MBHI, allowing for a direct comparison of the utility of these two tests in predicting outcome. Patients were followed for 12 to 50 months. Results with the MBHI showed no scale elevations that were associated with poor outcome. On the other hand, the MMPI scales *Hs, D, Hy, Pt,* and *F* were significantly higher in the fair/poor outcome group than in the good outcome group.

Taken together, the results of research on the MBHI show that it is of little value in predicting the outcome of spine surgery. However, the direct relevance of MBHI items to health care attitudes may make it more valuable for developing and individualizing treatments that facilitate spine surgery outcome. Suggestions for such a use of the MBHI are given in chapter 6.

SCL-90. The final personality instrument finding widespread use with back pain patients is the SCL-90 (Derogatis, 1977) and its more recent version, the SCL-90R. This is a 90-item inventory that assesses distress on nine different scales: *somatization, obsessive–compulsive, interpersonal sensitivity, depression, anxiety, hostility, phobic anxiety, paranoid ideation,* and *psychoticism.* A global symptom index is also generated. Studies with chronic pain patients have shown that there are basically three distinct profiles that emerge (Shutty & DeGood, 1987; Williams, Urban, Keefe, Shutty, & France, 1995). Essentially, these can be characterized as patients having high, moderate, or low levels of psychological distress. Williams et al. (1995) found that the high distress group reported the highest levels of pain and depression and also displayed the lowest activity levels. However, Kinney, Gatchel, and Mayer (1991) found that the MMPI was a much more sensitive device for identifying psychopathology among chronic pain patients.

There are no published studies on the use of the SCL-90 as a presurgical screening device, so that elevated scores on this test cannot be considered a risk factor for poor outcome. However, this test has one clear advantage over the MMPI and even over the MBHI—its brevity. At 90 items, the test can be rapidly administered and scored. Further, because it is so brief, the SCL-90 may be more acceptable to the spine pain patient. In addition, SCL-90 research just reported suggests that it may be a useful tool for screening patient's overall level of psychopathology or distress (Kinney et al., 1991). Thus, when the physician is uncertain whether to order a complete PPS, or when little time exists for testing, the SCL-90 provides good information about the surgery candidate's overall emotional condition.

Summary of Personality Testing

Of the three major personality tests that have been applied to spine pain populations, only the MMPI has substantial research support as a predictor of surgical outcome. However, each of these tests has its own strengths and weakness. These are summarized in Table 5.3.

Testing for Cognitive Factors

Perhaps no area in pain management has attracted as much attention in recent years as has the assessment of cognitive factors. Such factors, which involve the way the patient thinks about and copes with the pain, have been

TABLE 5.3
Strengths and Weakness of Personality Tests in the Assessment of Spine Surgery Candidates

Test	Strengths	Weaknesses
MMPI-2	Strong research support	Lengthy (567 items)
	Wealth of descriptive personality information	Normed on psychiatric population
	Widely recognized as "gold standard" personality test	May be objectionable to some patients
MBHI	Assesses personality in relation to medical problems	Minimal research support in relation to surgical outcome
	Moderate length (150 items)	Less widely recognized than MMPI
	Excellent suggestions for facilitating outcome	
SCL-90	Very brief (90 items)	No research on surgical outcome prediction
	Good screen for global psychological distress	Not designed for medical population
	Substantial research on chronic pain patients	Provides minimal details of personality

found to underlie many aspects of pain and injury. Cognitive factors significantly influence the patient's adjustment to pain, emotional status, and motivation for improvement. Rehabilitation of chronic pain patients is substantially improved by the inclusion of techniques aimed at altering cognitive processes (cognitive–behavioral intervention; see Turner & Jensen, 1993). Furthermore, chronic pain patients who display major gains through rehabilitation tend to have a significant reduction in negatively biased cognitions (Jensen et al., 1994).

A major review by Jensen, Turner, and Romano (1991) examined the results of published studies on cognitive factors in chronic pain. This literature review identified two major sets of cognitive factors that can influence adjustment to chronic pain: pain-coping strategies (29 studies) and pain-related beliefs (62 studies). *Coping* refers to specific thoughts and behaviors people use to manage their pain or their emotional reactions to pain (G. Brown & Nicassio, 1987). *Beliefs* are the thoughts patients have regarding either the consequences of having pain or their ability to cope with the pain. Both coping strategies and pain-related beliefs may influence the outcome of spine surgery.

Coping With Pain

There are a number of questionnaires that purport to assess pain-coping techniques, including the Vanderbilt Pain Management Inventory (VPMI; G. Brown & Nicassio, 1987), the Ways of Coping Checklist (Folkman & Lazarus, 1985), and others (see Jensen et al., 1991). Of the pain-coping devices, however, the coping strategies questionnaire (CSQ; Rosensteil & Keefe, 1983) has been the most widely researched in the area of chronic pain. Furthermore, the only cognitive measure that has been examined in relation to spine surgery outcome is the CSQ (Gross, 1986).

The CSQ defines seven cognitive and two behavioral coping techniques, as well as ratings of coping effectiveness (Table 5.4). The *cognitive techniques* can be described as internal dialogues that influence the way the patient perceives and responds to the pain. The *behavioral techniques* are overt activities designed to reduce the influence of pain sensations.

The CSQ has been used with many chronic pain patient populations, including osteoarthritis (Keefe et al., 1987), rheumatoid arthritis (Revenson & Felton, 1989), low back pain (Estlander, 1989; Keefe, Crisson, Urban, & Williams, 1990), myofascial pain (Keefe & Dolan, 1986), and general

TABLE 5.4
Coping Strategies Questionnaire Subscales

Cognitive Coping Strategies

    Diverting attention: thinking of things that serve to distract one away from the pain

    Reinterpreting pain sensations: imagining something that, if real, would be inconsistent with the experience of pain

    Coping self-statements: telling oneself that one can cope with the pain

    Ignoring pain sensations: denying that the pain hurts of affects one in any way

    Praying or hoping: telling oneself to hope and pray that the pain will get better someday

    Catastrophizing: negative self-statements, catastrophizing thoughts and ideation

Behavioral Coping Strategies

    Increasing activity level: engaging in active behaviors that divert one's attention away from the pain

    Increasing pain behavior: overt pain behaviors that reduce pain sensations

    Effectiveness Ratings

    Control over pain

    Ability to decrease pain

Note. From Rosenstiel and Keefe (1983)

chronic pain populations. Generally, these studies have proceeded by performing a factor analysis of CSQ scales, combining the individual scales into two or three factors. These rules for combining scales vary from study to study. However, Lawson, Reesor, Keefe, and Turner (1990) suggested the CSQ contains three basic dimensions: Conscious Cognitive Coping (including the *ignoring pain* and *coping self-statements* scales), Self-Efficacy Beliefs (including the *ability to control* and *ability to decrease* pain scales), and Pain Avoidance (including the *diverting attention* and *hoping and praying* scales). Although the results of this research are difficult to summarize, the most consistent finding, as noted by Jensen et al. (1991) is that Self-Efficacy Beliefs are frequently associated with lower pain intensity and greater physical functioning.

Much of the inconsistency in CSQ findings may be accounted for by the fact the pain populations being study vary widely, such that effective pain coping strategies may vary between syndromes. For example, Keefe and Dolan (1986) examined differences in CSQ responses between low back pain and myofascial pain patients. They found that the low back pain patients were much more likely to endorse "attention diversion," and "hoping and praying," as coping strategies than were the myofascial pain patients. The low back pain patients were also less active, took more narcotics, and showed higher levels of pain behavior. They concluded, based on earlier research (Rosenstiel & Keefe, 1983), that attention diversion, as well as hoping and praying, are "maladaptive," because they indicate that patients "have great difficulty accepting the fact that their pain will be chronic, and are (therefore) prone to cycle through periods of overactivity followed by increased pain and prolonged inactivity" (p. 55).

In a study directly relevant to PPS, Gross (1986) gave the CSQ preoperatively to 50 laminectomy patients. Outcome was measured in terms of pain intensity, sleep disturbance, and patient-rated surgical outcome. A factor analysis of the CSQ was performed, resulting in three factors: loss of control (combining low scores on the control dimension and high scores on the catastrophizing dimension), active coping and suppression (combining the coping self-statements, attention diversion, increased activities, ignoring and reinterpreting dimensions), and self-reliance (combining low scores on hoping and praying, with high scores on the pain control dimensions). Results of the study show that loss of control was negatively associated with postsurgical pain and positively associated with patient-rated surgical outcome. Self-reliance was negatively associated with postsurgical pain and sleep disturbance, and positively associated with surgical outcome. Active coping and suppression was not related to outcome. In other words, patients who responded well to surgery were those who felt some control over the pain, and also felt they could rely on themselves to overcome the pain.

This CSQ result may seem somewhat surprising. Patients receiving spine surgery have essentially decided that they cannot "live with the pain" and rely on the surgeon to remove or repair its source. Thus, it may appear that they are resigning themselves to the fact that they can not control the pain. However, for the spine surgery candidate, the operation is only the beginning of a long process of recovery and rehabilitation. This process relies on the patient's motivation and development of strategies to push for improvements in function despite pain. It may be that the most successful surgery candidates are those who are able to capitalize on the surgery by using their own pain control techniques. Thus, self-reliance and pain control ability seem to be associated with good surgical outcome.

The CSQ research strongly points to strategies that emphasize self-control as predictors of good surgical outcome. Such a notion also receives support from research on chronic pain patients using the other widely employed cognitive questionnaire, the VPMI. This is a 21-item test in which the patient endorses items indicative of "active" or "passive" pain-coping techniques. Active techniques include items such as "reading," "ignoring the pain," "engaging in physical exercise or physical therapy," and "clearing the mind of bothersome thoughts." These active techniques bear great similarity to the "self-reliance" and "pain control" factors based on the CSQ. Passive strategies from the VPMI include items such as "praying for relief," "taking medication for purposes of immediate pain relief," and "restricting social activities." Examining chronic pain patients, G. Brown and Nicassio (1987) found that active coping was associated with reports of decreased pain, lower depression, and less functional impairment.

As of the mid-1990s, only the Gross (1986) study, reported earlier, has directly examined the influence of coping strategies on surgical outcome. However, based on this study, as well as the chronic pain literature, poor pain control and a low sense of self-reliance should be considered risk factors for poor surgical outcome. It is recommended that these be assessed either through the CSQ self-reliance and pain control factors, or through the VPMI passive coping strategies dimension.

Pain-Related Beliefs

From a cognitive–behavioral perspective, the patient's pain-related beliefs should have a significant impact on both emotional status and the use of pain-coping strategies. That is, the way in which the patient understands and interprets his or her injury influences the patient's progress in pain treatment.

The sheer volume of research on pain-related beliefs is somewhat overwhelming. A review by Jensen et al. (1991) identified 62 belief-related studies on chronic pain, utilizing a great number of different belief assessment devices. Many more studies have been conducted since Jensen et al.'s review. As of 1996, the more frequently used belief-related devices are the Cognitive Evaluation Questionnaire (Phillips, 1989), the Survey of Pain Attitudes (SOPA; Jensen & Karoly, 1991), the Fear-Avoidance Beliefs Questionnaire (Waddell, Newton, Henderson, Sommerville, & Main, 1993) and the Pain and Impairment Relationship Scale (Riley, Ahern, & Follick, 1988). None of these beliefs questionnaires have been applied systematically to spine surgery candidates. However, the results of pain-belief research on chronic pain populations may have application to surgical patients. Some of the major findings from this literature, and recommendations for assessment are discussed here.

Locus of Control.   One can believe that pain sensations are under one's own control (internal locus of control) or that the pain is uncontrollable except by outside events, such as medication or surgery (external locus of control). Internal locus of control has been found to be associated with lower pain levels, less pain-related interference with functioning (Rudy, Kerns, & Turk, 1988), and lower levels of depression (Skevington, 1983). Although a number of locus of control instruments exist, the Multidimensional Health Locus of Control Scale (Wallston, Wallston, & De Vellis, 1978) is recommended.

Cognitive Errors.   A cognitive error is a negatively distorted belief that one holds about oneself or one's situation. Many types of cognitive errors have been defined in the clinical and research literature (see McMullin, 1985). Some examples of these errors are:

Overgeneralization: seeing a single negative event as a never ending pattern of defeat.

Personalization: seeing oneself as the cause of some negative event over which one has had no influence.

Catastrophizing: misinterpreting a minor setback event as a catastrophe.

All-or-None Thinking: seeing things only in black or white terms.

Emotional Reasoning: assuming that one's negative feelings about a situation must be true.

Many studies have been conducted examining cognitive errors in relation to the experience of chronic pain. For example, Keefe, Brown, Wallston, and Caldwell (1989) found that, among arthritis patients, catastrophizing was associated with high pain intensity, high levels of depression, and low physical functioning. Similarly, Gil, Abrams, Phillips, and Keefe (1990), examining sickle cell, rheumatoid arthritis, and chronic pain patients found that higher reports of negative self-statements (such as "I am useless" and "I am a burden on my family") were associated with greater pain and greater psychological distress.

Jensen et al. (1991) suggested that cognitive errors may predict long-term adjustment to chronic pain. Therefore, it may be useful, especially for treatment planning purposes, to include some measure of cognitive errors in the PPS. Suggested devices for such assessments are the Cognitive Error Questionnaire (CEQ; Lefevbre, 1981) and the Inventory of Negative Thoughts in Response to Pain (Gil et al., 1990).

Self-Efficacy.   Bandura (1977) suggested self-efficacy as a critical belief in dealing with stress. *Self-efficacy beliefs* may be defined as expectancies that one has the ability to engage in a specific stress-relieving behavior, and that this behavior will produce positive results. When one has such self-efficacy beliefs, the likelihood of engaging in the coping behavior increases.

The concept of *self-efficacy* has been applied to chronic pain. It has been suggested that patients engage in specific types of pain-coping behaviors, such as physical exercise, biofeedback, or hypnosis, to the extent that they believe they can perform these behaviors and that the behaviors will either reduce the pain or improve their functioning. The research on self-efficacy in chronic pain is quite exciting. Recent studies have shown that self-efficacy beliefs are associated with exercise performance during rehabilitation (Dolce, Crocker, Moletteire, & Doleys, 1986), with ability to perform activities of daily living (O'Leary, Shoor, Lorig, & Holman, 1988) and better overall adjustment.

Estlander, Vanharanta, Moneta, and Kavinto (1994), studying low back pain patients, assessed the relationship of self-efficacy to performance on a standardized measure of strength and effort, isokinetic testing. To assess self-efficacy, they constructed a questionnaire in which they listed eight activities (such as walking, running, or carrying weights of 4–5 kg in both hands) and asked the patient how long he or she felt it was possible to endure each activity. They found that self-efficacy expectations displayed a more significant association with the isokinetic test results than did the patient's pain level or self-rating of disability.

Self-efficacy beliefs seem to offer great potential as a component of PPS, although such beliefs have not been researched on surgical candidates up to this point. In surgical candidates, feelings of self-efficacy could be assessed in regard to pain control techniques (such as hypnosis, relaxation techniques, or biofeedback), physical exercise, abilities to reduce pain medication, and other behaviors important for postsurgical rehabilitation. For treatment planning purposes, self-efficacy questionnaires such as those developed by Keefe, Brown, Wallston, and Caldwell (1990) or Jensen et al. (1991) may be modified to assess the spine surgery candidate. Also suggested is the SOPA (Jensen, Karoly, & Huger, 1987), examines aspects of self-efficacy, along with other beliefs such as those about pain control, solicitude, disability, medication, and medical cure.

Avoidance.   Anyone who has back pain quickly learns that the pain can be reduced by limiting activities. However, a number of authors have observed that "patients' perception of physical activity and its relation to pain, and also their perception of their physical capabilities is often quite erroneous" (Waddell et al., 1993, p. 161). Such erroneous thoughts are termed *fear-avoidance* beliefs. Waddell et al. (1993) found that such beliefs, assessed by the Fear-Avoidance Beliefs Questionnaire, explain a large portion of the variance in functional activities of low back pain patients. Those patients who held strong beliefs that they would be harmed by pain displayed much lower levels in activities of daily living, and had greater work loss than did patients without such beliefs. Similar results have been obtained by Riley et al. (1988), using the Pain and Impairment Relationship Scale (PAIRS).

Fear-avoidance beliefs among spine surgery candidates are difficult to interpret. In many cases of patients with surgical lesions it may well be true that specific physical activities could create a worsening of pathophysiology. Furthermore, once the patient has been informed of the potential need for surgery, he or she might be expected to decrease activity in anticipation of the surgical procedure. Fear-avoidance beliefs, therefore, are probably not as critical an influence on surgical outcome as they are on the outcome of chronic pain management programs.

A Comment of Cognitive Assessment

This section on assessment of cognitive factors leads to a number of conclusions. First, there are very few studies directly examining the influence of cognitive factors on spine surgery outcome. Second, there are a tremendous number of questionnaires assessing cognitive factors in chronic pain. Finally, there is a great deal of overlap in the cognitive concepts assessed by these questionnaires. For example, "self-efficacy" and "internal locus of control" both examine the patient's self-confidence in controlling and overcoming pain.

Given the paucity of research on surgical outcome and the complexity of interpreting cognitive questionnaires it is recommended that no more than two devices assessing cognitive factors be used. Based on its research support, the CSQ (Rosenstiel & Keefe, 1983) is strongly recommended for assessment of pain-coping techniques. For treatment planning purposes, we recommend the additional use of a well-validated pain belief inventory (such as the SOPA or the CEQ).

Summary of Psychometric Predictors for Poor Surgical Outcome

The risk factors for poor surgical outcome identified in psychometric testing are listed in Table 5.5. These are combined with psychological risk factors identified during the interview to determine the overall level of psychological risk (see chapter 6).

TABLE 5.5
Psychological Risk Factors for Poor Surgical Outcome Identified From Psychometric Testing

Risk Factor	Risk Level
MMPI-2 elevations (*T* score > 70)[*]	
Single-Scale Elevations	
Scale 1–*Hypochondriasis*	High risk
Scale 3–*Hysteria*	High risk
Scale 2–*Depression* (preexisting)	High risk
Scale 2–*Depression* (reactive)	Moderate risk
Scale 4–*Psychopathic deviate*	High risk
Scale 7–*Psychasthenia*	Moderate risk
Coping Strategies Questionnaire	
Low self-reliance	High risk
Poor pain control	High risk

[*]In using the MMPI, the practitioner should observe the risk levels associated with the two greatest elevations seen on the profile (refer to chapter 6).

Tips for Psychometric Testing

The following suggestions are offered for the effective and appropriate use of psychometric testing in PPS.

Explain the Rationale for Psychometric Testing.   As has frequently been noted in this practice guide, the spine surgery candidate may be taken aback by the PPS. This can be especially true of psychometric testing devices, such as the MMPI. It is helpful to explain to the patient that the tests constitute another way to get to know the patient and how he or she is affected by the pain. It can also give the surgeon some indications of problems that may influence recovery from spine injury, so that these can be taken into account in developing and individualizing treatment plans.

Administer Testing After the Interview.   By allowing rapport to develop during the interview, and by providing some insight into the value of psychological assessment as part of the presurgery screening process, the patient is more likely to be compliant, motivated, and truthful in responding to the testing.

Use Testing as Part of a Comprehensive Evaluation.   Psychometric testing should never be given in the absence of a diagnostic interview when the data may be used to deny surgery to a patient. There are simply too many other factors affecting surgical outcome and too many possible explanations for scale elevations that can only be assessed during the interview. The only exception to this rule would be when a relatively simple test, such as the SCL-90, is used to screen patients in order to determine whether a complete psychological evaluation is indicated.

Review Test Results With the Patient.   After having spent a great deal of time and energy, as well as perhaps having overcome initial resistance, the patient is usually quite interested in the results of the testing. Butcher (1990) noted that providing test feedback is both a therapist's duty and an excellent approach to beginning psychotherapy. It is strongly recommended that the test results be presented to the patient in the context of the PPS feedback session (see chapter 6), during which the patient is informed of surgical prognosis and treatment plans are developed.

Summary

Psychometric testing is a critical component of the PPS process. Testing can both assist in describing characteristics of the patient and in predicting treatment outcome. Furthermore, testing can serve as a check on the accuracy of the practitioner's judgment. The MMPI, in particular, has been well researched as a predictor of spine surgery outcome, and is highly recommended as a component of PPS. The Coping Strategies Questionnaire is also especially useful. Other tests, such as the MBHI, and certain pain-belief tests, such as the SOPA or the CEQ can be very helpful for treatment planning purposes. By combining psychometric testing with the results of the interview, and with medical information, the practitioner is able to generate a clear, concise, and scientifically justifiable outcome prognosis and treatment plan.

Chapter 6

PPS Decision-Making: Determining Prognosis and Planning Treatment

The information included in the previous chapters provided the behavioral health practitioner with road maps on the quest for data affecting the outcome of spine surgery. Means for identifying patient risk factors through the review of medical records, a semistructured interview, and psychometric testing have been elucidated. At this point, the practitioner has completed the data-gathering phase and is able to reach two sets of conclusions. First, a concise and scientifically justifiable prediction of surgical outcome may now be determined. Second, individualized treatment plans can be developed for facilitating surgical results, for gathering additional data, or for providing treatment alternatives to surgery.

The integration of PPS data in order to reach these conclusions involves science, compassion, and expertise. Often, conflicting pieces of information and contradictory emotions create strong dilemmas in the practitioner's decision-making process. The practitioner frequently must weigh the patient's strong expressed desire to eliminate pain against the high level of risk factors identified. The surgeon's enthusiasm for the operation may clash with the patient's strong tendencies toward pain sensitivity or narcotic dependency. And always, lurking in the background, is the possibility of litigation over some perceived incorrect decision.

It is the purpose of this chapter to help the practitioner deal with these difficulties by providing clear guidance in the decision-making process. A procedure for determining surgical prognosis is given. This procedure is based on cataloging identified risk factors, and then applying clinical judgments and expertise, within a specified framework. Methods for developing treatment pathways are also detailed. With these guidelines, the practitioner should be able to feel comfortable, secure, and justified in the conclusions of the PPS.

Determining Prognosis

Determining surgical prognosis involves a process of scientifically weighing evidence. The evaluator examines all the patient's strengths and weaknesses in regard to back pain and coping with surgery. If the patient's history, current status, and psychological functioning show enough positive signs, the patient should be considered an appropriate surgical candidate. It is, however, unwise, to proceed with invasive spine surgery in a patient who appears to have a great many risk factors.

In recent years, the spine surgery weighing process has been examined in a number of studies. These studies have involved creating "scorecards," which catalogue and quantify data, ending up with a single spine surgery outcome prediction score. For example, the original scorecard, developed by Finneson and Cooper (1979), listed both positive and negative factors influencing the outcome of spine surgery. Positive factors included items such as "sciatica more severe than back pain" and "positive straight leg raising," whereas negative factors included items such as "gross obesity," "poor psychological background," and "secondary gain." Positive and negative points were awarded for each factor identified. Higher positive point totals appeared to be associated with better outcome at follow-up 3.8 years postsurgery. Similar scorecards, developed by Spengler et al. (1990) and Junge et al. (1995) showed that patients with a high level of identified risk factors have poorer outcomes in terms of functional abilities, vocational status, narcotic consumption, and need for additional surgery.

The PPS Scale

This practice guide also uses a scorecard approach to summarizing information obtained in the PPS. Our device, the PPS scale, is displayed in Fig. 6.1. This scorecard differs from others in two ways. First, the PPS scale

Name: _____	Oswestry _____	Date _____
Med DX: _____	Onset _____	ID _____
MD: _____	Surg. Type _____	Psych _____

Medical	Risk	Interview	Risk	Testing	Risk
Chronicity		**Litig./SSDI**		**MMPI (T>70)**	
6-12 mos	med	present	high	(max. 4 points)	
> 12 mos	high	**Work Comp**			
Prev. Spine Surg.		working	med	*Hs*	high
One	med	non working	high	*D* (pre-inj.)	high
Two +	high	**Job Disatis**		*D* (reactive)	med
Destructiveness		moderate	med	*Hy*	high
Min-Mod	med	extreme	high	*Pd*	high
Highly	high	**Heavy Job**		*Pt*	med
Salvage	high	>50 lb lift	high		
Non organic		**Sub. Abuse**		**CSQ**	
Present	high	pre injury	med	(max. 2 points)	
Non spine Med		current	high		
moderate	med	**Family Rein.**		low self-rel	high
multiple	high	moderate	med	low cont.	high
Smoking		extreme	high		
< 1 pack/day	med	**Mar. Disatis.**			
> 1 pack/day	high	present	med		
Obesity		**Abuse**		**Test Total**	_____
>50% over	med	pre injury	med		
		current	high	**Psych total**	
Med Total	_____	**Pre injury Psy**		**(Int. + Test)**	_____
Threshold	= 8 ± 2	outpatient	med	**Threshold =**	**10 ± 3**
		inpatient	high		
MED RISK = ____		**INTER TOT.** ____		**PSYCH RISK** = ____	

PROGNOSIS	MED TREATMENT RECOMMENDATIONS
GOOD	Clear for surgery, no psych necessary
FAIR	Clear for surgery, post-op psych
POOR	Hold, pending psych intervention
	Do not operate, conservative care only
	Do not operate, recommend discharge

FIG. 6.1.   PPS risk factor summary sheet.

provides for much more detailed and specific analysis of psychological factors influencing spine treatment outcome. Second, the PPS scale permits the inclusion of clinical judgment in the decision-making process. This is accomplished by identifying a quantified threshold for both high psycho-logical and medical risk, but allowing the practitioner to exercise clinical judgment when the patient's risk is close to that threshold (see later). In so doing, the scientific basis of the PPS scale is retained, while it also incorporates the practitioner's insights about the patient.

Determining Prognosis

The PPS scale is designed for ease of use, simplicity of communication, and scientific justification of decision making. As can be seen in Fig. 6.1, the PPS scale includes all the medical risk factors (see Table 3.4) and psychological risk factors (see Tables 4.1 and 5.5) identified earlier in this text. Each factor listed on the PPS risk sheet is identified as carrying either low, medium, or high risk. Points are assigned to each level of risk. Each high-risk factor is assigned 2 points, each medium risk factor 1 point, and each low-risk factor zero points. In the lower left-hand corner of the PPS scale is the succinct conclusion of all the practitioner's effort—the patient is declared to have a good, fair, or poor prognosis. The referring physician, then, can simply read this conclusion or may scan the PPS scale to identify the salient factors in the decision-making process.

The steps involved in using the PPS scale to determine surgical prognosis and to arrive at a set of treatment recommendations are as follows:

1. Identify risk factors: After gathering all data through review of medical records, interview, and psychometric testing, the practitioner cir-cles the identified individual risk factors on the PPS scale form. It is also important to note the demographic data at the top of the form.

2. Obtain total medical and psychological risk: Total risk scores are derived by addition. To obtain the total level of medical risk, the points in the medical risk column are added. The total number of psychological risk points involves a slightly more complicated process. The total psychologi-cal risk is composed of interview and testing points. The interview points are obtained by summing the risk factors in the interview column. For psychometric testing, the rule is that the patient can only score points for two elevations on the MMPI and one scale on the CSQ, for a maximum of 6 points. These testing points are then added to the interview points to determine the total psychological risk level.

If the practitioner has not gathered information about a factor listed on the PPS scale this should be noted and the patient receives 0.5 points for that item.

3. Determine whether risks exceed threshold: Once the total medical and psychological risk points are derived, each is compared to its respective threshold level. The patient is considered to have a high level of medical risk if the medical point total exceeds the threshold of 8 points. The client is considered to have a high level of psychological risk if the psychological point total is above the threshold of 10 points.

4. Apply clinical judgments in cases of near-threshold risk scores: The practitioner can choose to place the patient on either the high or low side of the risk threshold if the total dimension score falls within the threshold range. The range is different for the medical and psychological risk factors:

- For the medical risk dimension the threshold range is a total score of 6 to 10 points (8 ± 2);
- For the psychological risk dimension the threshold range is a total score of 7 to 13 points (10 ± 3).

5. Determine surgical prognosis: The patient's surgical prognosis is determined by the level of psychological and medical risk, as seen in Fig. 6.2 (compare to Fig. 1.1). Patients who have a low level of both medical and psychological risk are considered to have a "good" prognosis. Those patients with one high-risk factor and one low-risk factor are considered to have a "fair" outcome prognosis. When both factors are high risk the patient is considered to have a "poor" prognosis.

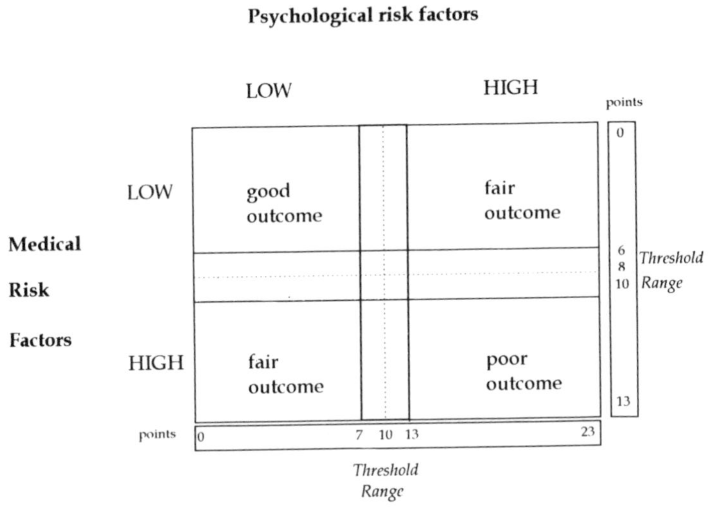

FIG. 6.2.   Spine surgery prognosis determined by medical and psychological risk factors.

Applying Clinical Judgment

The determination of surgical prognosis is often straightforward. Some patients have a clear, uncomplicated medical picture with minimal psychological distress, leading the practitioner to easily conclude that the patient has a "good" prognosis. Other the other hand, a "poor" prognosis is easily determined when the patient has extreme psychological difficulties and cloudy medical picture full of risk factors. However, the determination of surgical prognosis is much more complicated when both the patient's psychological and medical problems fall into a moderate range (i.e., close to the established high-risk thresholds). In such cases, the practitioner is faced with a dilemma: Decision making must be tied to data, but an overreliance on firm threshold may force the practitioner into a decision with which he or she strongly disagrees.

In order to illustrate this dilemma, consider several examples. First, consider the patient just under the threshold for psychological risk who has such a strong history of narcotic addiction that the practitioner feels this single problem could easily reoccur, negatively impacting outcome. Allowing for surgical clearance could lead to failure by creating a situation that capitalizes on the patient's tendencies for drug dependence. On the other hand, consider a patient who has had multiple spine surgeries leading to a number of additional risk factors, such as medication dependence, a high anger level (seen as an elevated score on the MMPI *Pd* scale), the breakup of a marriage, and so forth. If these multiple spine surgeries are explainable as resulting from iatrogenic causes, such as infection or failure of instrumentation, then one might be inclined to think of the patient as having a reasonably good surgical prognosis.

Factors Influencing the Use of Clinical Judgment

There are a number of issues involved in a case that may cause one to raise or lower the risk threshold. Many of these are subtle and are developed as the practitioner gains experience with the use of PPS. However, the following suggestions may be helpful as a starting point in applying clinical judgments to moderate risk patients.

Examine the Strength of Specific Identified Risk Factors

Risk factors are treated on the PPS scale in categorical fashion, that is, as present/absent or high/medium/low risk. Although such categorical decisions simplify the PPS process, for certain risk factors the full possible range of a problem is ignored. For example, consider the "destructiveness" medical risk factor. On this factor, a patient has a high-risk level regardless of whether the proposed surgery is a one-level uninstrumented fusion or a three-level circumferential fusion with hardware. Similarly, in assessing MMPI *Hy* scale elevations, no distinction is made on the PPS between patients who have a *T* score of 71 and those who have a *T* score of 100. One might wish to lower the total risk threshold and place the patient in a high total medical or psychological risk category to the extent that the patient has several specific factors with very high levels.

Examine Extenuating Circumstances

Although the patient may have sufficient identified risk factors so that the total score falls in the threshold area, there are often explanations for such factors that would argue against their representing a true risk. For example, some iatrogenic problems, such as severe depression leading to psychiatric hospitalization, may result from many causes not attributable to the patient. A thoughtless physician might maintain the patient without any significant treatment on a high level of narcotics for months or even years. A long-term employee may be terminated from his or her job shortly after being injured and suffer severe financial consequences. When plausible, extenuating circumstances account for some of the risk factors, the practitioner may wish to slightly raise the threshold and place the patient in a low-risk medical or psychological category.

Note Problematic Behaviors

Surgical candidates may demonstrate behaviors that can interfere with their ability to recovery from surgery and their interactions with health care providers. Such behaviors may be observed during the interview, they may be revealed through review of medical records, or the treating physician may report problems with the patient. Some behaviors that might lead to a marginal candidate being placed in a high-risk category are:

- Noncompliance: often observed as a history of frequent missed appointments or unwillingness to carry out treatment plans.
- Staff-Splitting: often observed when the patient complains about other staff members, relates improbable information given by other health care providers, or idealizes the practitioner.
- Manipulation and demands: often observed when the patient attempts to get the behavioral health practitioner to act in inappropriate ways, for

example, by convincing the surgeon to dispense more medication, or by assisting the patient's attorney in a lawsuit.

- "Extortion:" often observed when the patient makes threats if his or her treatment demands are not met. For example, the patient threatens to sue the surgeon if no operation is forthcoming. Sometimes a patient may even threaten suicide if surgery is denied.
- Drug-seeking behavior: often observed not only by early demands for refills, but also by doctor shopping for prescriptions, calling in after hours, frequent emergency room visits, etc.
- Defeatist attitude: often observed when the patient believes that no intervention will be helpful, that the surgeon is uncaring, or that no solutions exist for the patient's problems.

There are obviously a number of other issues that might cause the practitioner to slightly lower or raise the risk threshold in a particular case. However, by only permitting such a change in threshold when the patient's risk factors scores are within a narrow range, the PPS scale provides a critical restriction on the use of clinical judgment in determining surgical prognosis.

Medical Treatment Recommendations

The PPS scale, as seen in Fig. 6.1, contains five different types of treatment recommendations. As described in chapter 1, these five recommendations follow from the patient's level of surgical prognosis. If the patient receives a "good" prognosis then he or she is considered clear for the possible operation. However, this recommendation can be either for unqualified surgical clearance, or for the inclusion of postoperative psychotherapy. If the patient receives a "fair" prognosis, surgical clearance is not necessarily given. The practitioner may opt to proceed with the operation but to include postoperative psychotherapy, or may place the patient on "hold" for surgery. In the hold condition, some interventions are recommended for reduction of risk prior to clearing the patient for surgery. Only if the patient shows responsiveness to these interventions is surgical clearance given. If the patient receives a "poor" prognosis, surgery is definitely contraindicated. In this case, the practitioner may either recommend that the patient receive a course of conservative treatment or may recommend immediate discharge. A suggested treatment plan format is given in Fig. 6.3.

Guidelines for determining medical treatment recommendations are discussed here.

Treatment Plan
Re:

Date of Plan

Problems:
1.
2.
3.
4.

Relationship of above listed problems to the patient's injury:

Interventions Planned:
1.
2.
3.
4.

Frequency of total treatments

Expected duration of total treatments

Expected clinical response to treatment

Specific re-evaluation timeframe

Treatment Justification:
This treatment plan is designed to :
have a positive effect on the patient's overall condition:
improve ability to return to or retain employment:

Treating Clinician:

FIG. 6.3.   Sample treatment plan form.

Good Surgical Prognosis: Unqualified Surgical Clearance Versus Postoperative Psychotherapy

When the patient is cleared for surgery with a good prognosis, the operation can proceed at any time. However, there may still be important postoperative mental health interventions that could be expected to improve surgical outcome. Such "facilitative" interventions center especially on reducing controllable risk factors. Interventions might be directed, for example, at smoking cessation, weight reduction, or programs for reduction of narcotic use. Similarly, other more psychological problems, such as depression or anger, could be the focus of postoperative intervention. Further, if a high level of marital dissatisfaction or significant spousal reinforcement of disability exists, then couples' counseling could be an important adjunct in the postoperative plan.

The rationale for postoperative psychological intervention in the patient cleared for surgery, then, rests on three significant points:

1. Some alterable risk factors are identified.
2. The client demonstrates motivation to deal with these problems (see chapter 3 for hints on motivational assessment).
3. Results can be obtained using a brief therapy approach of 10 sessions or less.

The importance of using brief therapy approaches cannot be overstated. Some patients, for example those with a strong history of sexual abuse, may require months or years of psychotherapy. Any postoperative intervention proposed should not be directed at resolving such long-term problems, but simply at improving circumscribable issues that might affect surgical outcome. This same admonition to use brief therapy techniques applies to all psychological treatment recommendations given in this practice guide.

Fair Surgical Prognosis: Postoperative Psychotherapy Versus Hold, Pending Outcome of Psychotherapy

The fair surgical candidate presents the practitioner with a dilemma. Patients who fall into this category have a significant number of risk factors and usually a number of these are alterable. The question is whether to recommend that the surgeon proceed with the operation along with any psychotherapy is undertaken ("clear for surgery") or whether some of these risk factors can and should be reduced prior to undergoing surgery ("hold on for surgery").

In some cases, this decision is relatively easy. When the patient's presentation and psychological testing reveal the presence of a psychological crisis such as severe clinical depression, preoperative treatment of this condition is warranted. High levels of narcotic consumption may also require reduction or detoxification prior to surgery. When the patient is currently a victim of physical or sexual abuse the situation needs to first be stabilized.

The decision to defer surgical clearance pending the outcome of psychological intervention becomes more difficult as problems are subtler.

The key points in making this decision are:

- The patient's history indicates noncompliance with medical regimens.
- Testing such as MMPI Hy and Hs elevations indicates a very high level of pain sensitivity.
- A high level of ambivalence about surgery is expressed by the patient or spouse.
- The fair risk patient engages in alterable problematic behaviors, such as smoking or heavy alcohol consumption, that could be controlled prior to surgery in order to improve outcome.

If the decision is made to defer surgery pending the outcome of psychological intervention, the practitioner must identify specific criteria as well as a definite time frame for reassessment of surgical status. The criteria for determination should relate to reduction in the targeted risk factors, such as elimination of smoking, reduction of narcotics to a specific level, or improvement in depression level. Generally, the time frame for reassessment should be no greater than 2 months. If the patient does not achieve sufficient reduction in risk factors within the specified time frame, then he or she should be considered for conservative care or discharge only.

Poor Surgical Prognosis:
Conservative Care Only Versus Discharge

The poor surgical candidate is one whom the practitioner has determined will not respond well to surgery. For these patients the practitioner is especially obligated to determine a course of action that may lead to improvements in the pain condition. By definition, these patients have a great many psychological and medical problems, so their treatment may be quite difficult and the outcome uncertain. However, as research in chronic pain programs (Block, 1982; Flor, Fydrich., & Turk 1992) have demonstrated, many of these patients can reduce pain levels and improve function with proper treatments.

Not all poor surgical candidates are appropriate for intervention. For some, the risk factors are simply so great as to be insurmountable. It is also the case, as discussed in chapter 3, that about 5% of spine pain patients may be malingering (i.e., consciously manufacturing symptoms). Treatment for such patients would be inappropriate and would unnecessarily inflate treatment costs. It is expected that about 80% of poor surgical candidates can benefit by some conservative treatment.

The key points in making the decision to recommend conservative care versus discharge are the following:

1. Extreme inconsistency in presentation, such that the patient reports high pain levels but displays low pain behaviors. The patient may also display very exaggerated behaviors, or a high level of pain behaviors when observed directly, but low pain behavior levels when observed unobtrusively. This extreme inconsistency may indicate malingering and would argue in favor of rapid discharge.
2. The patient states that a large financial gain is expected as a result of the injury.
3. The patient has previously failed an interdisciplinary pain management program.
4. The patient has expressed highly negative attitude or anger toward treatment staff or physicians. Patient may also express no desire toward a pain program and that it would only amount to "going through the motions."

Psychological Treatment Recommendations

The surgical prognosis and medical treatment recommendations often call for the inclusion of psychological intervention, either preoperatively, postoperatively, or as alternatives to surgery. Psychological interventions in the context of the spine surgery are similar to those used with chronic pain patients. In general these interventions are symptom oriented, specific, or brief.

It is not the purpose of this text to provide detailed psychological treatment descriptions. The reader is referred to several very useful texts for such descriptions (Barber & Adrian, 1985; Tollison, 1989). However, the following are offered as suggestions for the four general areas targeted by psychological interventions in spine surgery candidates.

Demonstrating and Improving Motivation and Compliance

Treatments with these goals are especially useful in the fair prognosis patient who is placed on hold pending the outcome of psychological intervention. These patients may have a history of noncompliance or may demonstrate questionable commitment to their own role in recovering from the back injury. If the patient makes a commitment and carries through on it, this bodes well for the outcome of invasive procedures. Some suggested motivation and compliance interventions are discussed here.

Medication Reduction Contracts. These contracts are especially useful in the patient with a history of drug-seeking behavior or the patient taking a high level of preoperative medication. Such contracts (see Fig. 6.4) can help to avoid many postoperative problems. Given the tendency of many patients to receive multiple prescriptions from different physicians, we recommend that the medication-dependent patient agree to periodic random

I, _____, recognize that many pain-relieving

medications have addicting properties. Therefore, I agree to control my use of

these medications. I agree that prior to surgery I will take no more than:

____ _____

   (#)   (medications)

per day. Surgery may be canceled if I take a higher level of medication.

I also recognize that narcotic medication may be a problem after surgery. If

surgery is undertaken I agree that I will gradually reduce my use of narcotics

quickly after surgery. ____ weeks after surgery I will be completely free of

narcotic medications.

_____   _____

Name   Witness

_____

Date

FIG. 6.4.   Sample medication contract.

urine or serum blood screens. In some cases, narcotic dependence may be so high as to require formal detoxification programs.

Pacing.   Many back pain patients have difficulties with pacing activities. Frequently patients in high demand jobs will take large doses of narcotic medication in order to cover their pain, so that they can work longer hours or exercise more. Such patients frequently have difficulties slowing down and use activity for purposes of stress relief. Of necessity, many of these patients will need to modulate activity levels postoperatively to allow themselves time to recover. It is recommended that such patients keep preoperative records of daily activities, exercises, and medication. Paced activities may get them used to a more relaxed lifestyle and force them into learning other stress-relieving skills. Surgery may need to be postponed or canceled if patients do not complete activity diaries or if pacing cannot be achieved.

Smoking Control.   As noted in chapter 2, smoking is associated with increased probability of disc problems, and with slower and more problematic outcome of fusion surgery. Preoperative reduction of smoking is, thus, both justified scientifically and can be used to demonstrate and improve the patients' motivation and compliance. Use of a nicotine patch or gum (Hughes, 1993), smoking control hypnotherapy, smoking reduction schedules (Cinciripini et al., 1995), or a combination is recommended.

Weight Reduction.   Obesity, as noted earlier, is only a moderate and relatively unproven risk factor for poor surgical outcome. However, in the patient of questionable motivation, or when the physician feels strongly that obesity will negatively influence outcome, weight reduction should become the target of pre- or postoperative psychological intervention. Weight control interventions have quite variable results and there is no standard recommended treatment. However, recent research shows that the combination of cognitive–behavioral intervention with low calorie liquid diets (Wadden, Foster, & Letizia, 1994) or with the provision of low calorie meals (Jeffery et al., 1993) can be effective in producing long-term weight loss. It is suggested that when weight control is recommended, the patient should be referred to a program using these or similar techniques.

Improving Mood

In chapter 5, it was noted that a patient's negative beliefs about the injury, pain, or about the ability to recover could adversely impact surgical outcome. Such beliefs involve external locus of control, cognitive errors, poor self-efficacy, and avoidance. These beliefs act to make the patient more depressed, immobilized, and hopeless. The treatments discussed here may be helpful in altering such negative beliefs and improving emotional status.

Antidepressant Medication.   Clinical depression is a common occurrence in spine surgery candidates. Perhaps this is because there is a great deal of overlap between the symptoms of pain and depression, including sleep disturbance, appetite impairment, decreased motivation, decreased sexual activity, social withdrawal, low self-esteem, and crying spells. For this reason, antidepressant medication may be quite beneficial for the spine surgery candidate. It is suggested that when the PPS reveals the presence of significant clinical depression (e.g., MMPI *D* score > 80), antidepressant medication should be given for 1 month prior to undergoing surgery. Such medication may have the additional benefit of providing some element of pain relief (Atkinson, 1989).

Cognitive–Behavioral Intervention.   Often, antidepressant medication is not sufficient to produce long-term improvements in motivation and emotional status. Such results often require some psychological intervention aimed at altering the patients pain-related beliefs. Numerous studies have shown that such cognitive–behavioral interventions are successful with chronic pain patients, producing improvements in functional ability and decreased health care utilization (Jensen et al., 1994) as well as reductions in self-reported pain (Keefe, Salley, & Lefevbre, 1992).

A number of cognitive–behavioral interventions exist (see McMullin, 1985, for an excellent practice guide). As these are applied to spine pain patients, they often involve identifying the patient's pattern of negative pain-related beliefs (see chapter 4) and the environmental triggers for such beliefs. The patient then works on developing a less negative, more adaptive set of beliefs in response to the environmental triggers.

Cognitive–behavioral techniques are best applied as a postoperative intervention. These techniques usually require multiple (up to 10) sessions and could delay otherwise necessary surgery. Furthermore, it may be difficult for the patient to develop a realistic, positive set of beliefs before the outcome of the surgery, in terms of pain relief and improved function, is known.

Teaching Pain-Coping Skills

All surgical candidates have some element of pathophysiology to account for their complaints. Yet the pain report may vary greatly—in intensity, frequency, and quality. There are undoubtedly some subtle physical elements that at least partially account for individual differences in pain reports between patients with similar injuries. However, as was reported in chapter 5, patients also vary in terms of "pain sensitivity." That is, some patients are more likely to report pain with a lower level of nociceptive input. Such pain-sensitive patients may benefit by a course of pre- or postoperative training in pain-coping skills.

Preoperatively, pain-coping skills may be used on patients whose pain reports seem disproportionate to their injuries, in order to determine how much control they can gain over pain. Often, once such patients have learned pain-coping skills, they find they have achieved sufficient control that they are less interested in having surgery.

Pain-coping skills training may also be critical for the spine surgery candidate. It is rarely the case that spine surgery leads to an elimination of all pain. Rather, a reduction in pain intensity is expected. Many patients may continue to have difficulty coping with even this reduced pain.

Hypnosis, Imagery, and Relaxation Training. Pain-coping skills training involves teaching the patient new ways to deal with noxious signals arising from the injury. There are many ways to achieve such pain control skills, including hypnosis (Hilgard & Hilgard, 1975; Sacerdote, 1982), relaxation techniques (Ter Kuile et al., 1994), and biofeedback (Keefe & Block, 1984). These techniques all make use of four types of skills, to varying degrees:

- Deep Muscle Relaxation: activation of the parasympathetic branch of the autonomic nervous system (ANS; Basmajian, 1983);
- Distraction: moving attention away from pain signals;
- Imagery: visual, kinesthetic, or other sensory foci for nonpain-related attention;
- Dissociation: the ability to separate normally connected mental processes, leading to feelings of detachment or distancing (Wright & Wright, 1987).

Some imagery and pain control techniques are listed in Fig. 6.5.

Coping skills approaches have, to various degrees been shown to be effective in reducing subjective pain sensations (Hilgard, 1978; Meier, Klucken, Soyka, & Bromm, 1993). Coping skills training has the additional advantage of confirming that the patient's pain experience has a physiological basis, while at same time demonstrating that these noxious sensations are controllable through the patients own efforts. Thus, the patient can also can experience an enhanced sense of self-efficacy.

Dissociation:	Separate the painful body part from the rest of your body, or imagine you body and mind as separate, with the pain distant from your mind.
Sensory Splitting:	Divide the sensation into parts. For example, if the pain feels hot or tingling to you, focus on the heat or tingling and not on the hurting.
Altered Focus:	Focus attention on nonpainful parts of the body (hand, foot, etc.) and alter sensation in that part of the body. For example, imagine your hand warming instead of focusing on the back pain.
Anesthesia:	Imagine an injection of numbing anesthetic (like Novocain) into the painful and surrounding areas.
Analgesia:	Imagine yourself getting an injection of morphine into the painful area. Or, imagine your brain producing massive amount of endorphin (the natural pain-relieving substance of the body).
Transfer:	Produce altered sensations—heat, cold, anesthetic, etc.—in a nonpainful hand, then place the hand on the painful area. Transfer this altered sensation into the painful area.
Age Progression/ Regression:	Use imagination to project yourself forward or backward in time to when you are pain-free, or experiencing much less pain. Then suggest you act "as if" this image were true.
Symbolic Imagery:	Imagine a symbol that represents a pain (such as a loud, irritating noise or a painfully bright light bulb). Gradually reduce the irritating qualities of this symbol (e.g., dim the light or reduce the volume of the noise), thereby reducing the pain.
Biofeedback Imagery:	Create an appropriate mental image linking biofeedback to pain control. For example, if attempting to reduce muscle tension headaches, you might imagine your neck or forehead muscles as a tight steel band or spring that relaxes as the tone on the feedback changes.
Positive Imagery:	Focus attention on a pleasant place that you could imagine going (the beach, mountains, etc.) where you feel carefree, safe, and relaxed.
Counting:	Silent counting is a good way to deal with pain episodes. You might count breaths, holes in an acoustic ceiling, floor tiles, or even mental images.
Pain Movement:	Moving pain from one area of your body to another, where the pain is easier to cope with. For example, move back pain slowly into the arm or hand.

FIG. 6.5.   Imagery and pain control techniques.

Dealing With Issues of Reinforcement for Pain

As noted in chapter 3, certain elements in the patient's social, economic, and vocational situation may act to reinforce pain or disability. Such reinforcement may make the probability of good surgical outcome less likely. Psychological intervention aimed at reducing the influence of reinforcement for pain can be directed at areas discussed here.

Family Reinforcement of Disability.   Research (Block, 1981; Lousberg et al., 1994) has shown that spouses or family members may reward pain behavior by providing the patient with solicitous attention for pain. Psychological intervention can help family members to recognize and alter their responses to pain. Family members need to examine their emotional, cognitive, and behavioral responses to the patient's pain behavior. They should learn to avoid soliciting pain behavior (i.e., not anticipate the pain or take over the patient's responsibilities, or dispense medications unnecessarily). They can also learn the importance of attending to the patient for "well behaviors" (i.e., behaviors not related to the pain or injury). They often may need to learn the importance of seeking support from the patient, as they would if the patient was not in pain, so that the patient does not feel patronized. Although it is inevitable and to some extent desirable for family members to take care of the spine pain patient, psychological intervention can minimize the untoward reinforcement of disability that may result. Such behaviorally oriented family therapy is appropriate before or after surgery.

Vocational Issues.   Spine pain patients often experience a high level of anger in relationship to their jobs. They may feel anger toward the employer for causing the injury (see chapter 5), or for lack of support once the injury has occurred. Patients may have their employment terminated due to a back injury, leading to a high level of anger, as well as vocational uncertainty. All these issues may strongly impact the patient's ability to recover.

Anger and other feelings relating to work are not easily nor quickly modifiable. Cognitive–behavioral intervention, including "reframing" of anger-producing situations, and "brainstorming" new solutions may be of value. Vocational counseling to explore the patients aptitudes and capitalize on strengths, can help the patient out of the malaise, suspiciousness, and low self-esteem that often accompany impending job termination. As all of these interventions require a significant investment of time, and may also rely on a concrete knowledge of the patient's functional ability level, therapy aimed at dealing with vocational issues should be undertaken in the postoperative period.

Financial Gain.   For many patients, the spine pain is the basis for legal action. Patients may sue the party who caused the injury. If the accident occurred at work, patients generally cannot sue their employers, but often look for third-party litigation. For example, a patient may bring action against the manufacturer of equipment that was involved in the injury. Even if no accident occurred, financial gain may flow from spine pain. This occurs when the patient seeks long-term disability benefits.

For many patients, the financial gains that follow from an injury are quite meager, especially in the case of job-related injuries. In most states, patients injured under worker's compensation receive weekly pay benefits equal to two-thirds of their preinjury wage. Even with tax breaks, the net income is rarely greater than 85% of preinjury wages. However, many worker's compensation patients may believe that they are in for a large settlement even if this is not a possibility. Disabusing patients of such beliefs, perhaps by referring the patient to a group discussion with other similar patients, may reduce the influence of such imagined financial gain, although the patient may then become more angry.

There are some patients who can expect to receive large settlements through the tort system for their injuries. In such cases, individual psychotherapy is recommended during the postoperative period. This therapy is aimed at helping the patient to understand that improvements in functional ability are important to self-esteem. Further, the settlement the patient receives is more related to the fact that a surgery has resulted than to whether he or she is able to perform specific activities, such as 10 or 15 repetitions of a trunk-strengthening exercise. By pointing out the negative aspects of disability, and by emphasizing the value of health and return to normalcy, the practitioner can overcome to some extent the disincentives associated with a legal settlement.

Interdisciplinary Pain Management Programs

As has frequently been noted throughout this book, interdisciplinary chronic pain management programs have been demonstrated to be effective in helping very recalcitrant patients acheive improvements in functional abilities, heightened mood, decreased pain, and diminished reliance on pain medication (Flor et al., 1992). Such programs generally involve psychological intervention (individual and group therapy), physical therapy, physical exercise and reconditioning, and occupational therapy. The psychological elements of such a program include the techniques listed above.

Interdisciplinary pain management programs may be especially valuable to two groups of PPS patients. First, those patients who are declared a poor surgical risk, but are still seen as amenable to treatment, will benefit by the array of interdisciplinary procedures. Second, those patients who are cleared for surgery, but have a lengthy history and risk factors in the threshold range, may need the depth and breadth of services provided in a chronic pain program. In fact, recent research by Rainville, Sobel, and Hartigan (1995) demonstrated that postsurgery patients who participated in such a program acheived significant improvements in functional capacities, such as lifting and pain-free straight-leg raising, as well as decreased depression levels, although pain levels were not significantly reduced.

Referral to an interdisciplinary pain management program, although expensive, may be the wisest option in dealing with some of the most difficult PPS patients.

Summary

PPS has involved gathering information through review of medical records, a semistructured interview, and psychometric testing. In this chapter, procedures are given for quantifying and combining the poor outcome risk factors in order to determine surgical prognosis. Techniques are also given for including clinical judgment in the decision-making process, when the patient has a moderate level of risk factors. The PPS scale allows for a succinct summary and set of medical treatment recommendations. Also given in this chapter are suggestions for pre- and postoperative psychological intervention, as well as for alternatives to surgical intervention.

Proper patient selection and the development of psychological treatment plans may be the keys maximizing surgical and conservative outcome, as well as to avoiding iatrogenic spine problems. Integrating the explicit PPS criteria using the procedures described in this chapter can, thus, be of great benefit to the patient, the surgeon, the employer, and insurance companies.

Chapter 7

PPS Reports

Having completed the PPS, the practitioner is confronted with issues of documentation. Behavioral health practitioners are quite well versed in writing evaluation reports, so that PPS documentation may seem to be a simple matter, at first glance. However, documenting the evaluation of a spine surgery candidate carries unique challenges, as well as responsibilities. The practitioner who attends to these documentation issues will produce reports that are, at once comprehensive, succinct, scientifically based and respectful of the patient's need for privacy.

PPS reports, it must be acknowledged, serve many purposes. For the physician, the primary interest is in obtaining an objective reading of the patient's psychological make-up, as well as receiving assistance in treatment planning. The insurance company may be most interested both in avoiding unnecessary surgery, and also in determining if any psychological problems are unrelated to or preexist the injury. Employers may want to know about the patient's psychological characteristics, in order to determine how these may impact the ability to work. Finally, the patient will certainly want to know how and why a behavioral health practitioner determines surgical prognosis and wields influence over the physician's decisions.

Each of the interested parties, the patient, surgeon, insurance company, and employer, may read PPS reports from their own perspective. It could easily be the case where wordy, vague, or unjustified statements could be misunderstood. Thus, reporting on specific PPS results requires, at once, scientific credibility and tactful communication. Credibility is strongest when one not only documents carefully the basis for decisions in specific cases, but also when each patient becomes a part of ongoing research on surgical outcome. Tactful communication follows from discussing the specific surgical prognosis and treatment plans within a context of both the patient's strengths and the benefits that follow from the recommended treatment plans.

The purpose of this chapter is to guide the practitioner in providing PPS reports. Suggestions are given for producing timely, succinct PPS written evaluations. Also, outlines for verbal feedback to the patient are given—the type of feedback varying by the patient's surgical prognosis. Finally, an outline for on-going PPS research is provided, with an eye toward demonstrating the validity of outcome predictions. This combination of attention to specific cases, integrated with clinical outcome-based investigations, will allow the practitioner to provide evaluations with sophistication, efficiency and scientific validity.

Reporting to the Physician

The practitioner who has completed a PPS has not performed a comprehensive psychological evaluation. Rather, very specific information that is relevant to a determination of surgical prognosis has been obtained. The PPS report, therefore, should not attempt, nor does it require, the level of psychological detail that most practitioners normally include in their initial evaluation notes. Further, one must consider that the primary audience for the evaluation is a busy physician, who ordinarily has neither the time nor the inclination to read a detailed psychological history.

Most physicians prefer reports that are quite succinct and clear-cut. In fact, it is often the case that simply sending the physician a completed copy of the PPS scale (see Fig. 5.1) is sufficient documentation for decision-making purposes. After all, this form can be completed quite rapidly and provides the scientific basis of all the practitioner's decisions. However, because many different individuals may read the PPS, a somewhat greater level of detail and justification for decisions must be present.

The following suggestions are offered in preparing PPS case reports:

- Be focused. Information reported should be relevant to the task at hand: surgical outcome prediction and planning for recovery from the back injury. Reporting in great detail on the patient's history adds little of value to these goals, and may add sensitive material to the PPS report. By remaining focused, the practitioner avoids unnecessary legal exposure, also.

- Use standardized reporting format. Free-form, dictated reports are sure to leave out some significant information and overemphasize other data. By using a standard reporting format the practitioner ensures all relevant information is identified and reported.
- Be succinct. Reports should generally run no more than four to five pages. Relevant risk factors should be clearly identified.
- Provide a brief summary and treatment plan at the end of the report. Physicians are accustomed to reading diagnostic reports from medical tests such as EMG, CT scan, and so on, which provide detailed information but conclude with a succinct set of findings and possible recommendations. In the PPS, therefore, physicians are likely to focus on the end of the report, because they may not have time to read the full report.
- Remember the medico–legal context of the report. The PPS report may become part of a legal action. The patient may sue the party who is responsible for the injury and the employer. A defendant in an action brought by the patient may subpoena the practitioner's records. The patient may even bring suit directly against the practitioner for the decisions made in the PPS. In writing the PPS report, therefore, the practitioner must carefully document all factors involved in the decision-making process and be prepared to defend these in court.

There are many possible reporting formats for PPS case reports. Figure 7.1 provides one such format, which adheres to the suggestions just given. This format has the advantage that it follows directly from the PPS scale form (Fig. 6.1) used to determine surgical prognosis. It, therefore, ensures documentation of all key risk factors. Certainly, practitioners may wish to modify this structured reporting format, or develop one of their own, in order to fit personal styles and preferences.

In addition to the PPS report, it is also wise to inform the physician or the physician's assistant verbally of the decision. There are several reasons for providing such supplemental verbal reports. First, the practitioner may be able to verbalize certain facts of the case that are better left out of the written report. These may be particularly confidential but relevant information such as current abuse by the spouse, anger at the physician, and so on. Second, the physician may have already scheduled surgery for the patient. If the PPS reveals a poor surgical prognosis the physician will likely cancel the surgery, leaving a hole in the surgical schedule. Rapid verbal feedback allows for another case to be substituted quickly. Finally, unfortunately, improper filing of reports or slow mail service may undo all the benefits to

Client:
Date of Screening:
Date of Testing:
Referral Source:
Proposed Surgery:
Insurance Type:

History of Symptoms:
Onset, blame for initial injury
Types and successes of conservative care, surgeries
Current medical diagnosis, if known
History of "doctor shopping"?

Pain Measures and Modifiers:
Present, average, highest, and lowest pain ratings
Events that exacerbate and reduce pain
Consistency of interview pain behavior with pain report

Reason for Seeking Treatment:
State that this is a PPS report

Other Major Medical Problems and History:
Non spine-related medical problems, especially hospitalizations

Function During a Typical Day:
Uptime, general activity level, feelings about activity

Sleep Disturbance:
Total sleep, periods of restlessness, cause for sleep disturbance
Does sleep disturbance pre date injury?
Recurrent dream themes

Energy Level
Is report of energy level change consistent with sleep disturbance?

Appetite Disturbance and Weight Change:
Change in weight
Is weight consistent with depression, reduced activity, etc?
How much overweight?

Memory and Concentration Difficulties:
Note short- and long-term impairments
Is cognitive impairment related to pain episodes?
If traumatically injured, is there a possible brain injury?
Is cognitive impairment consistent with depression?

Subjective Mood Experience
Feelings of anger, depression, anxiety
Cognitions during these emotional periods
Suicidal, homicidal thoughts
Physiologic response to these moods
Crying spells

Employment History:
Employment duration at time of injury
Type of job and job demands
Job satisfaction, attitude
Employment stability
Post operative vocational plans

Educational Background:
Is current employment consistent with educational background

Marital and Family:
Duration of current significant relationship
Satisfaction with relationship
Response of family to pain behavior
Abuse
Support network

Prior Psychiatric or Psychological Treatment:
Previous inpatient and outpatient hospitalization
Pre injury psych history?
Causes of previous psych problems
Currently receiving treatment?

Medications and Substance Use:
Narcotics and analgesics
Psychotropics & other medications
Smoking and alcohol use
Street drugs
Substance abuse history
Current medication compliance problems

Legal Issues and Social Security Disability:
Litigation pending and expectations for outcome
Applying for or receiving social security disability

Expectations for Treatment Outcome:
Expectations realistic (some, but not complete relief of pain)
Sense of self-responsibility for improvement
Recognition of need for pacing and compliance in affecting outcome

Mental Status:
Formal mental status not usually required but should note:
appearance, cognition, mood, observable pain behaviors and their consistency
with pain report
Use of any appliances, such as wheelchair, TENS unit, etc.

Personality Measures-_MMPI (suggested):
Focus on MMPI elevations, as detailed in chapter 4, relating to surgery outcome
Other scale elevations related to treatment planning

Cognitive Coping Measures--Coping Strategies Questionnaire (suggested):
Focus on self-reliance, control as related to outcome
Other scales in relationship to treatment planning

Cognitive Belief Measures--SOPA, Cognitive Errors Questionnaire, etc.
Identify negative beliefs that may be target for psych intervention

Other Test Results:
Suggest no more than two additional brief questionnaires relevant to treatment
planning.

GENERAL CONCLUSIONS:

(This section on a separate page)

Major Psychological Symptoms:
  Current active problems, stated in bullet fashion

Relationship of Psychological Symptoms to Pain and/or Injury:
  Do psych problems predate or result from injury?
  Are pre-existing psych problems exacerbated by injury?
  Do psych problems affect pain-related functioning or recovery?

Psychological Strengths:
  Coping skills, past history of overcoming problems
  General positive features in patient's presentation
Psychological Liabilities:
  Pain sensitivity
  Poor coping skills and negative beliefs
  General problem features of case
Psychological Treatment Plan:
  Explicit statement of pre- or post-op psych treatments
  Goals for treatment
  Expected treatment duration
Medical Treatment Recommendations & Client Management Suggestions:
  Surgical clearance and prognosis
  Suggestions for medical staff about patient management
  Necessity for psych intervention

Diagnoses:
  Axis 1:
  Axis 2:
  Axis 3 (Medical diagnosis):
  Axis 4 (Current stresses):
  Axis 5: Current GAF: Highest GAF in past year:

Signature Block

FIG. 7.1.   PPS: structured case reporting format.

the practitioner of timely, accurate written reports. Thus, both the practitioner and the surgeon are well served by providing both verbal and written PPS reports.

Informing the Patient

The PPS not only serves to render a surgical prognosis and develop a treatment plan, but also to both inform and to educate the patient about areas that may negatively impact the outcome of intervention. Most often, patients have a great deal of respect for the insights and suggestions of the well-trained behavioral health practitioner. Furthermore, the patient invests both a great deal of time and reveals a tremendous amount of very intimate information during the PPS. It is the responsibility of the practitioner to match the patient's level of commitment by tactfully and authoritatively providing feedback about the PPS.

The following general suggestions are given for informing the patient about PPS results.

Schedule a Separate Feedback Session, If at All Possible

Informing the patient of PPS results at the time of the initial interview is to be avoided, for a number of reasons. First, even the highly experienced practitioner may find that his or her initial impression of the patient changes a bit on reflection. For example, subtle, nonverbal indications of excessive pain sensitivity or negative attitudes may not be fully realized until one writes the PPS report. Further, the interview or testing may bring up issues, such as noncompliance or anger, which may necessitate either a closer reading of the medical record or additional discussion with the referring physician. Finally, it is often the case that complete psychometric test results may not be available at the time of the interview. Making PPS decisions and informing the patient in the absence of such results is dangerous. As was noted in chapter 6, test results not infrequently contradict the practitioner's impressions, requiring a review of the results with the patient. Delaying the PPS feedback session allows the practitioner to fully incorporate all important information into the decision-making process.

Be Circumspect, Especially if a Delayed Feedback Session is Not Possible

Unfortunately, time does not always allow for a delayed feedback session. Despite educating the physician about the importance of performing the PPS early in the presurgical work-up, this may be logistically impractical for a number of reasons. Thus, the patient may only be able to come once for the PPS, or the PPS may need to be conducted within just a few days of the scheduled surgery. When there is no opportunity to delay the feedback session, it is still important to provide the patient with information and education.

The immediate feedback session should begin by informing the patient that the results are preliminary and may change somewhat on further reflection. The practitioner should briefly review identified risk factors. A preliminary surgical prognosis can be given. Preliminary plans for addressing these risk factors should be given. The patient should be told that a more complete written report, which will be available at a later date, will be developed.

Be Tactful and Positive

Although the PPS focuses on identifying risk factors for poor surgical outcome, the practitioner's report to the patient should begin by emphasizing the patient's strengths. The practitioner should acknowledge the patient's identified positive pain- and stress-coping strategies. The practitioner should look for other positive aspects of the patient's presentation, including minimal use of medication or strong social support. Even the patient's ability to avoid severe depression in the face of pain can be turned into a event deserving of praise.

Report on Identified Risk Factors, But Normalize Them

All presurgical candidates present with a problem that they believe may be at least partially solved by a surgeon. However, the risk factors identified may make such a solution either improbable or highly unlikely. Even in the patient who has been cleared for surgery, addressing risk factors in some fashion can improve the odds of a good outcome. The manner in which the practitioner presents these risk factors can determine whether the patient works on solving these problems or is defensive, and does not accept the practitioner's perspective.

The practitioner should use the feedback session to report the major, alterable risk factors that have been identified during the PPS. These risk factors should not be reported in an accusatory fashion, but rather in a spirit of concern. Further, whenever possible, the practitioner should normalize identified risk factors. That is, it can be explained to the patient that many of the problems he or she is experiencing are common in spine surgery candidates. As examples, depression is experienced in up to 80% of chronic back pain sufferers, and medication dependence is also very common. It is also perfectly natural to feel anger toward the employer in an on-the-job injury, although this emotion is not particularly helpful as far as surgical outcome is concerned. By presenting identified risk factors in a caring fashion, and normalizing those factors, the practitioner is preparing the patient to deal with these difficulties productively.

Report Surgical Prognosis as the Result of Careful and Comprehensive Evaluation

Having identified problematic aspects of the case, the practitioner should then report on surgical prognosis. Several points should be kept in mind in giving such a report.

- This prognosis is based on comprehensive evaluation of medical records, interview, and testing data.
- The surgeon is the ultimate decision maker and can accept or reject the practitioner's opinion.
- The practitioner should describe specifically how identified risk factors can have a negative influence on outcome.
- By determining surgical prognosis, the practitioner is helping the patient to maximize the opportunity to benefit from treatment and to avoid treatments that are unlikely to be successful.

This last point is particularly important. Many patients are aware of the mixed results of spine surgery. The patient who is cleared for surgery as a result of the evaluation can receive a great deal of assurance from this fact: Because psychological risk factors have been found to have a such a strong influence on spine surgery outcome, passing the PPS greatly improves the odds of a good outcome. The candidate placed on hold pending treatment outcome, can be made more aware of the importance of addressing risk factors. Even the patient who is not cleared for surgery may be pleased with the outcome of the PPS, if a proper explanation of the risk factors is given. Such a patient can be shown that by avoiding spine surgery one avoids heading down a road of increasingly difficult operations that are unlikely to have beneficial results. Alternatives to spine surgery exist, either through formal treatment or self-help, and the patient who is not cleared for surgery may be able to benefit by these.

Help the Patient Find Solutions
to Identified Risk Factors

The key to improving surgical outcome is for the patient to address and resolve, as much as possible, problems that may have a negative effect on outcome. The type of plan for risk-factor resolution depends on the patient's surgical prognosis.

Patients Cleared for Surgery, No Psychological Treatment Necessary. In such cases there may be some problems that should receive attention by the patient in order to best recover from the surgery. The patient can be given a list of community or self-help resources for dealing with these difficulties. For example, self-help books can provide ways to improve mood, marital distress, or overcome some aspects of an abuse history. Community resources such as state vocational rehabilitation services, churches, or social service agencies can help significantly to improve the patient's psychosocial difficulties. Pointing these patients in these directions has the additional positive effect of increasing the patient's self-responsibility for improvement.

Patients Cleared for Surgery, Postoperative Psychotherapy Recommended. Patients who fall into this category will almost certainly obtain better surgical outcome if they receive effective psychological intervention. It is the job of the practitioner to help the patient become motivated and committed to such a course. It is important in such cases that the patient recognizes and takes ownership of behavioral and emotional problems. In order to facilitate these goals, during the feedback session the practitioner should help the patient to identify how these problems have a daily effect on either the patient's ability to achieve life goals or on general feelings of adjustment and self-worth. Brainstorming with the patient approaches to resolving these difficulties is an excellent way of motivating the patient for a course of postoperative psychotherapy.

The patient's motivation for postoperative psychotherapy can also be increased by tying treatment of psychological problems to improved surgical results. For example, unresolved depression may increase pain sensitivity. Similarly, marital upheaval may create a high stress level, taking the patient's focus away from postoperative rehabilitation. By dealing with these identified risk factors, the patient will be doing everything possible to minimize such difficulties and improve the odds of obtaining pain relief.

Patients Placed on Hold, Pending the Outcome of Psychological Intervention. For these patients, the therapist needs to be quite directive. Not only does the practitioner need to provide a strong rationale for psychological treatment, but the patient also needs to know that surgery cannot proceed without both commitment to reducing these risk factors and a demonstration of improvement. Rather than brainstorming solutions, the practitioner should give explicit treatment guidelines. Furthermore, criteria for treatment success should be given. As examples, it might be explained that a history of previous noncompliance makes it necessary for the patient to demonstrate strict adherence to a schedule of exercise or medication reduction in the preoperative period. Excessive medication intake, missing appointments, or avoidance of assignments will result in the practitioner recommending against surgery. Similarly, the patient may be required to take antidepressant medication for 4 to 6 weeks preoperatively in order to improve motivation and decrease pain sensitivity. Preoperative cognitive–behavioral intervention may be required to reduce displaced anger or to develop more realistic expectations of surgical outcome. Only if the patient addresses and resolves these identified risk factors will the practitioner clear the patient for surgery.

Patients With Poor Prognosis, Conservative Care Only. These patients may be very confused by the practitioner's decision to recommend against surgery. Often, at one level, they see surgery as the only way to resolve pain. However, the therapist can often be successful in helping such patients see noninvasive treatment as the preferable option. It should be pointed out that the results of spine surgery are far from uniform and that the PPS has revealed a very high number of risk factors. Rather than proceeding down a course of invasive intervention, which is fraught with problematic outcome and the possibility of further surgery, the patient has the opportunity to minimize pain and improve functional ability through his or her own efforts, in concert with the guidance of treatment staff. An interdisciplinary program, which addresses pain control, increased strength and endurance, vocational issues, and education often can be as effective as surgery in the long-run, and can avoid additional pain in the short-run.

Patients With Poor Prognosis, Discharge Recommended. The therapist obviously, may feel the greatest reluctance to provide such patients with face-to-face feedback. However, such internal resistance should be overcome, as the feedback session provides several important opportunities. Careful explication of risk factors and their overwhelmingly negative impact on surgical outcome can help the patient recognize emotional and behavioral difficulties and accept a course of no further active treatment. Additionally, such a risk-factor review can minimize future medico–legal problems. Often, the patient will agree that he or she does not really desire surgery and that conservative treatment is ineffective. The therapist can then suggest self-help and community-based resources, similar to those suggested for the patient who is cleared for surgery with no psychological treatment recommended.

Provide a Written PPS Summary

A simple written review should be given to the patient at the end of the feedback session. This report should list some of major identified risk factors, surgical prognosis, and treatment plans. The written feedback review can be valuable in many ways. It ensures that the therapist has communicated the basis of decision making. It provides a definition of problems to be resolved. It describes specific plans for helping the patient to overcome difficulties that might negatively impact surgical outcome. Figure 7.2 represents a general patient PPS feedback that can accomplish these goals.

PPS Research Reports

The decision concerning surgical clearance has profound effects. Inaccurately declaring a patient to have a poor prognosis may condemn him or her to unnecessary, protracted pain and disability. Similarly, recommending that a poor surgical candidate receive an operation may reduce the surgeon's overall effectiveness and create a patient who is dependent and drug-seeking. The insurance company, too, suffers when inappropriate spine surgery is performed, for such treatment may lead to significantly increased direct and indirect medical expense. Thus, it is critical that the practitioner make correct projections of spine surgery outcome.

The practitioner who provides PPS has both the opportunity and the obligation to demonstrate the accuracy and effectiveness of these procedures. Clinical research is the vehicle for such demonstrations, and should become an integral component of PPS. PPS research can determine whether patients who have differing prognoses actually obtain different clinical outcomes. Furthermore, it can serve a descriptive purpose, documenting emotional, behavioral, and medical differences between patients in the three prognostic groups. Finally, PPS cost-effectiveness can also be documented.

Because the PPS prognostic decision is based on primarily objective, quantified data, examination of the accuracy of these decisions is simply a matter of having a general research plan and accurate record-keeping. Suggestions for developing and maintaining on-going PPS research begin on page 123.

Patient Name: _____   Date: _____

Referring Physician: _____   Medical Diagnosis: _____

Thank you for participating in the Presurgical Psychological Evaluation. As you are aware, this is a routine procedure designed to maximize your opportunity to recover from a spine injury. The Presurgical Psychological Evaluation has involved a review of your medical records, an interview and psychological testing. Based on this comprehensive evaluation we have reached the following conclusions:

Your major strengths and assets in dealing with the spine injury:

     1.

     2.

     3.

Major risk factors which may have a negative impact on surgical outcome:

     1.

     2.

     3.

Your surgical outcome prognosis based on this evaluation (circle one):

     Good   Fair   Poor

General treatment recommendations to your physician (check one):

     ___ Clear for surgery, no psychological treatment recommended
     ___ Clear for surgery, post operative psychotherapy recommended
     ___ Recommend hold on surgery, pending the result of further treatment
     ___ Recommend conservative (non operative) treatment
     ___ Recommend no further treatment

Recommendations to improve emotional condition and other problems:

    1.

    2.

    3.

Desired results of psychological treatment

    1.

    2.

    3.

We will re-evaluate your status at the following time (for patients on hold):

Sincerely Yours,

FIG. 7.2.   PPS: patient feedback form.

Establish a Database

The foundation of good clinical research is accurate, objective clinical data. PPS procedures lend themselves to gathering analyzable data, particularly through the PPS summary sheet (see Fig. 6.1). This summary sheet reduces much qualitative information to a quantitative or numerical level. For example, marital dissatisfaction and job attitude are given values of 1 or 2 points on the PPS scale, depending on the intensity of the patient's reported experience. Having such quantitative data allows one to statistically analyze PPS results.

The most effective method for cataloging PPS data is to use a computer database program, entering the scores for each of the items, on completion of the PPS summary sheet. It is highly recommended that one not accumulate the data and enter a large number of patients into the database at one time, as this is a lengthy, and correspondingly burdensome process. A statistical consultant may be of value in establishing this computer database.

Determine Outcome Measures to Be Used

The predictive accuracy of PPS decisions is best documented by examining the progress of patients in the three prognostic groups. In order to measure progress, one must have documentation of how the patient is feeling and functioning, both at the time of the PPS, and at some follow-up interval. Pre–post comparisons can then be made to determine PPS predictive accuracy.

As noted in chapters 3 and 4, PPS outcome research often involves some variant of the Stauffer and Coventry (1972) criteria. These criteria examine four major areas: pain perception, work ability, functional ability, and continued medical care. Although many research studies have assessed outcome through the use of global provider judgments, it is most accurate and effective to use validated outcome measurement instruments, which are given to the patient's in pre–post fashion. Some outcome measurement recommendations are discussed here.

Pain Perception.   The patient's pain experience can be measured in a number of ways. The simplest technique is to use Likert-type scales. This simplest of these is a visual pain analog scale (VPAS), such as the following:

"Please rate your current level of pain on the following scale"

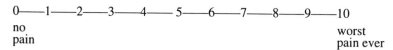

0——1——2——3——4—— 5——6——7——8——9——10
no   worst
pain   pain ever

In addition, the patient can be asked to rate average daily level of pain during the last week, as well as highest and lowest pain levels.

A more detailed assessment of the patient's pain perception can be obtained through the use of the McGill Pain questionnaire (MPQ; Melzack, 1975). This questionnaire contains lists of adjectives describing qualitative aspects of the patient's pain, along three dimensions: sensory, affective, and evaluative. In addition, the patient rates the intensity of pain sensation. This questionnaire has been widely utilized and well validated as an effective instrument for tracking outcome of pain management. Unfortunately, unlike the VPAS which takes just a few seconds to complete, the completion time for the MPQ may be about 5 minutes.

Functional Status.   The patient's ability to carry out self-care, vocational and recreational activities may be severely impaired by a back injury. Spine surgery should lead to significant improvement in such functional areas. There are two major functional activity scales in current use with spine pain patients. The Oswestry Disability index (Fairbank, Couper, Davies, & O'Brien, 1980) is a 10-item questionnaire, specific to spine pain, that provides quantitative assessment of activity in a number of different functional areas. This questionnaire has been shown to provide a sensitive assessment of pain treatment effects. Little and MacDonald (1994) showed that the Oswestry Disability index can also provide a good assessment of spine surgery outcome. The other widely used tool is the SF-36 (also available from National Computer Systems as the Health Status Questionnaire). This tool is being widely used in a broad range of medical conditions to track treatment-related improvements in functional activity. Although the SF-36 is not specific to spine injuries, its use can allow comparisons with established values for improvement in these other conditions. Additional functional ability scales for back pain, such as the Roland Disability Scale (Roland & Morris, 1983) are reviewed by Kopec and Esdaile (1995).

Additional Measures. It also recommended that the practitioner track outcome in a number of other relevant factors, through the use of a questionnaire. Items that can be included in such a questionnaire include:

- continued use of medications
- additional medical treatments and surgeries
- return to work, either full or limited duty
- enrollment in vocational retraining program
- ratings of satisfaction with treatment outcome
- global ratings of mood states, such as depression, anger, or anxiety

Obtain Outcome Measures at Regular Intervals

All measures to be used for assessing outcome, such as the Oswestry, the MPQ, or other more specific measures, should be given to the patient both at the time of the PPS and at regular follow-up intervals. Generally, sufficient information is gathered by obtaining assessment at 3 months, 1 year, 2 years, and 5 years post-PPS.

Obtaining follow-up information is not easy and may be time consuming. It must be remembered that:

1. Follow-up questionnaires should be mailed at the standardized intervals.

2. Patients who do not return questionnaires should receive a phone interview during which questionnaire items are asked. The individual conducting the phone interview should be well trained and be prepared not only to gather specific research information needed, but also to discuss problems the patient is having in dealing with the pain.

3. Expect that response rate will drop with increasing time from the initial PPS. Thus, although one may expect 60% to 75% of patients to respond at the initial follow-up, by 2 years the response rate may drop to 40% or 50%.

4. Offer the patient the opportunity to obtain research results when they are available. This can be an inducement for the patient, who must spend considerable time answering the follow-up questionnaires.

Analyze Between-Group Differences at Baseline and at Follow-Up Intervals

The goal of PPS research is to demonstrate that surgical prognosis predicts patient outcome. In order to determine such predictive ability, it should first be established that there are minimal baseline differences in outcome measures between patients in the three prognostic groups. That is, at the time of the initial PPS, patients in the good, fair, and poor prognosis groups should show similar average levels of functioning and pain sensation. Absent such a demonstration of no baseline differences, it is difficult to determine the significance of differences at follow-up. For example, consider the situation that occurs if patients in the good prognosis group have significantly better Oswestry scores at follow-up than do patients in the poor group. Without knowledge of initial Oswestry scores, one cannot say that the good prognosis patients showed any greater improvement than did the poor patients, for the two groups may have been different all along. Of course, the three prognosis groups should be expected to be highly different on items contained in the PPS scales, such as age, chronicity, medication use, and so on. However, aside from these PPS scale items, patients in the three prognostic groups should be shown to be quite similar.

One can assess baseline differences statistically, using simple tests (Anastasi, 1994). Overall between-group differences on numerical data, such as Oswestry scores or pain analog ratings, can be assessed with a simple t test. Qualitative or categorical data, such as whether the patient is taking narcotics or whether the patient is working, can be assessed using χ^2 test. In either case, a significance level of $p < .05$ should be used. If no between-group baseline differences on outcome measures are obtained, one is in a powerful position to show that PPS prognostic predicts response to treatment.

Assess Change Scores on Outcome Measures

At follow-up, patients in the three prognostic groups should show very different responses to treatment. This can be demonstrated by analyzing "change scores." Such scores are obtained by subtracting each patient's score at follow-up from the initial score. For example, a patient who reports a Level 9 pain at baseline and a Level 5 pain at follow-up would have a change score of 4. Notice that increases in pain above baseline would produce a negative change score. Such change scores can then be tested statistically, using t tests or χ^2 tests as in baseline comparisons.

The reader may recognize one problem with this analysis of difference in response to treatment between patients in the three prognostic groups. If patients obtain a poor prognosis as a result of the PPS they should not have surgery. Thus, it would be impossible to demonstrate that poor prognosis patients have a worse response to surgery than do patients with more sanguine prognoses. However, in actuality, it will undoubtedly be the case that the surgeon will sometimes choose to operate on patients even though they have obtained a poor PPS prognosis. These patients should be followed closely, for their results can firmly establish the credibility of PPS procedures. Furthermore, it is interesting to compare poor prognosis patients who receive surgery with poor prognosis patients who do not receive surgery. Statistical results can determine whether it is better to leave such patients untreated rather than subject them to possibly doomed operative procedures.

Other Interesting PPS Outcome Studies

There are almost an infinite number of ways PPS results can be statistically analyzed. As one becomes more familiar with the data, new lines of research suggest themselves. Two additional, relatively simple studies are discussed here.

Reduced Medical Cost (Medical Offset) as a Result of PPS.   S p i n e surgery is very expensive. Frymoyer and Cats-Baril (1987) estimated that the total hospital inpatient cost for back pain in 1990 was almost $6.8 billion, and the physician inpatient cost was another $1.7 billion. Unfortunately, good estimates of the cost of specific surgeries are hard to obtain. The following are general costs associated with different operative procedures in practices with which I have been associated:

- Discectomy: $18,000
- One-level posterior lumbar interbody fusion: $28,000
- Three-level circumferential fusion with instrumentation: $40,000

These costs include operative treatment, including diagnostic procedures, surgery, hospitalization and postoperative rehabilitation.

If one keeps track of the proposed operative procedures for all PPS patients, it is possible to determine the medical offset (cost savings) as a result of poor surgical patients avoiding surgery. Our own results, on the first 165 PPS patients analyzed, show that there were 32 who obtained poor prognoses. Of these, 26 did not have surgery. The medical offset was determined by estimating the total surgical treatment cost (based on the type of surgery planned) and subtracting from it the total cost for the 26 PPSs. The medical offset total for these 26 patients was an astounding $459,000.

Determining Between-Group Differences on Individual PPS Scale Items. It is quite interesting to determine in what ways patients from the three prognostic groups differ. One can analyze these differences in order to obtain hints at factors that significantly influence surgical outcome. For example, one may examine MMPI profile differences between prognostic groups, or differences in chronicity or substance abuse. Displaying such individual item differences can further validate the effectiveness of PPS in choosing those patients who should respond poorly to surgery.

Summary and Conclusions

PPS is a procedure that can have great value for the patient, the surgeon the insurance company, and even the scientific community. However, each of these beneficiaries requires different types of information and different reporting procedures. In this chapter, guidelines have been given for writing PPS reports to the referring physician, bearing in mind the medico–legal context of the reports. Specific guidelines have been given for reporting PPS results to the patient, so that motivation for improvement is maximized. Finally, some simple research designs have been suggested that can document PPS effectiveness and serve to market procedures to insurance companies. By both carefully documenting individual PPS results, and critically examining the effectiveness of PPS as a predictor of surgical outcome, the behavioral health practitioner is contributing to the credibility and acceptance of this procedure as a significant component of the spine surgery diagnostic process.

PPS offers the practitioner the unusual opportunity to provide a simple, low-cost, scientifically sound assessment process with profound effects. PPS can serve to strengthen the results obtained by surgery and avoid operative procedures for patients with little chance of good response. It can help the patient gain insight, motivate him or her to take responsibility for recovery from a back injury, and allow the patient to utilize and augment inner strengths in dealing with pain. It can produce significant cost savings for insurance companies and employers. It is our hope that by utilizing the procedures outlined in this practice guide, PPS will become firmly established as a critical component of the diagnostic process in spine surgery.

Chapter 8

General Applications of PPS in Chronic Pain Syndromes

Back pain is the most prevalent type of a wide variety of chronic pain syndromes. In almost every area of the body there exist numerous conditions associated with protracted pain experience. The International Association for the Study of Pain's (IASP) Pain Classification (Merskey & Bogduk, 1994) scheme lists literally hundreds of different chronic pain syndromes. For many of these, the primary treatment is conservative, and symptoms resolve without invasive procedures. However, in many chronic pain syndromes the treatment of last resort is often surgical. For example, carpal tunnel syndrome, a very common disorder associated with protracted numbness and stinging pain in the fingers, may be treated by surgery designed to release compression on the median nerve in the wrist, if physical therapy and splinting are ineffective. Similarly, trigeminal neuralgia, a fairly frequent condition involving sharp paroxysmal pain along the three branches of the trigeminal nerves, may eventually be treated by microsurgical decompression of the nerve root.

The literature on spine surgery, as reviewed in this practice guide, suggests that in many of these and other cases of chronic pain, PPS might be of value in assessing the surgical candidate. Certainly, any experience of protracted pain may lead to some of the same problems as have been found in back pain: excessive narcotic use, deconditioning syndrome (chapter 3), and inability to work, to name a few. Further, patients' personality dispositions and emotional states, and histories may affect their perception of, and response to, pain and injury. Thus, it seems likely that PPS may reveal
130

factors that militate against good surgical outcome in a broad range of chronic pain syndromes.

It is the premise of this chapter that PPS should be obtained when the patient is being considered for elective surgery if the primary purpose of the surgery is pain relief, and the pain has persisted for more than 6 months.

In this chapter, some of the same factors identified as carrying risk in spine surgery are examined in two other pain syndromes: chronic idiopathic pelvic pain (CPP), and chronic pain associated with the temporomandibular joint dysfunction (TMD). As is seen, many of the same psychological and behavioral factors are found in all three pain syndromes. This suggests that in many chronic pain syndromes, the efficacy of surgical intervention aimed at pain relief may be affected by emotional and behavioral issues. The chapter concludes with an outline of a general approach to PPS, which may be employed across a broad range of chronic pain conditions.

Screening the CPP Patient for Hysterectomy

Back pain may be the most common chronic pain syndrome, but the volume of spine surgery procedures pales in comparison to hysterectomy. As reported in chapter 1, approximately 280,000 low back surgeries are performed each year. Carlson et al. (1993), citing data from the National Hospital Discharge Survey (1992), reported that approximately 590,000 hysterectomies are performed each year in the United States. By the age of 60, more than 30% of U.S. women have undergone hysterectomy and the annual costs for hysterectomy are estimated to exceed $5 billion (National Center for Health Statistics, Pokras, & Hufnagel, 1987).

There are many accepted indications for hysterectomy. The majority of these indications are for primary reasons other than pain control, such as uterine cysts, dysfunctional uterine bleeding, genital prolapse, and endometriosis (Carlson et al., 1993). Protracted pain is often associated with these conditions, and the hysterectomy frequently provides pain relief.

Approximately 10% to 12% of patients who undergo hysterectomy (i.e., about 70,000 patients per year) have a primary diagnosis of CPP (N. Lee, Dicken, Rubin, & Ory, 1984). CPP is a nonspecific term, referring more to protracted pain duration than to particular diagnoses. In fact, many CPP patients have no laparoscopically identifiable pathology (Reiter, 1990).

Some patients (approximately 45%) may have nongynecologic pathology (such as irritable bowel syndrome and myofascial syndrome), whereas in the remainder, no organic pathology can be determined.

The category of women with no physical findings to account for their complaints is the one of most concern. Studies vary widely in the range of patients who are found to have negative laparoscopy results. Although reports range from 9% to 80%, with no identifiable pathology (Kresch, Seifer, Sachs, & Barrese, 1984; Levitan, Eibschitz, deVries, & Hakim, 1985), it is generally accepted that approximately 30% of patients who undergo laparoscopy will have no visible pelvic pathology (Slocumb, 1990a).

Baker and Symonds (1992) showed that up to 60% of CPP patients with negative laparoscopy results are pain free at 6-month follow-up. Yet, those CPP patients who continue to complain of pain may be considered for hysterectomy.

It is perhaps not surprising that pain relief after hysterectomy in CPP patients is far from uniform. Stovall, Ling, and Crawford (1990) reported that 22% of CPP patients have persistent pelvic pain after hysterectomy. Similarly, Slocumb (1990a) noted that one in five patients treated at his pelvic pain clinic have previously received a hysterectomy for CPP. Thus, it appears that hysterectomy for relief of pelvic pain can have quite variable results.

The outcomes obtained in hysterectomy for CPP are similar to those obtained in fusion and discectomy patients. For example, as reported in chapter 1, approximately 25% to 35% of patients who receive lumbar fusion continue to have pain after surgery (Turner et al., 1992). Although there may be many reasons for this similarity in outcome, one possible explanation is that many CPP patients have significant psychological and emotional difficulties. Just as is the case with chronic back pain, these difficulties can be expected to affect pain perception, motivation, and response to surgical intervention.

Risk Factors Associated With CPP

The literature on psychological factors associated with CPP is not nearly as complete, nor as scientifically grounded, as is the case in chronic back pain. Far fewer studies exist in CPP, and most do not examine the specific relationship between psychological factors and outcome of hysterectomy. Rather, there are two typical research designs. Some studies compare the psychological characteristics of CPP patients without laparoscopically identifiable pathology to patients with identifiable pathology (Rosenthal et al., 1984) or to normal patients (e.g., Reiter & Gambone, 1990). Others simply examine psychological, behavioral and emotional issues among CPP patients (e.g., Ryan, Dennerstein, & Pepperell, 1989; E. Walker, Katon, Neraas, Jemelka, & Massoth, 1992). Some of the factors associated with CPP are discussed next.

Multiple Nongynecologic Medical Complaints.   CPP patients tend to have a history of multiple physical complaints, as well as treatments and surgeries of a nongynecologic nature. Reiter and Gambone (1990) compared CPP patients to pain-free women who were undergoing routine annual examinations. The CPP patients had five times as many cumulative nongynecologic operations. Patients were also asked to identify current physical symptoms using a checklist procedure. The average number of symptoms among CPP patients was 7.9 versus 2 for controls. In a somewhat similar study, E. Walker et al. (1988) found that CPP patients had a significantly greater number of somatic symptoms than did a comparison group of normal controls.

Steege and Stout (1991) also conducted a relevant study of women undergoing laparoscopic lysis of pelvic adhesions. These patients would not fit the definition of CPP as used in this practice guide because they all had at least some level of identifiable pelvic pathology (the laparoscopically identifiable adhesions). However, Steege and Stout established their own definition of CPP. Patients were declared to have CPP if four of the following five criteria were present:

1. Pain duration greater than 6 months.
2. Incomplete relief by previous treatment.
3. Impaired physical functioning.
4. At least one vegetative sign of depression.
5. Altered family roles.

Using these criteria, CPP patients were found to have a higher number of prior operations than were non-CPP patients. The authors followed the patients for an average of 8.2 months post-lysis of adhesions. In this study, 40% of CPP patients reported improvement in pain at follow-up compared to 75% of non-CPP patients.

As noted in chapter 3, a high number of previous nonrelated medical complaints and operations is associated with poorer outcome of spine surgery. This association of multiple physical symptoms with poor outcome would appear equally applicable to hysterectomy.

Medication Use and Substance Dependence.   Patients with CPP tend to take a high level of medication and to be somewhat frequent users of drugs and alcohol. Walker et al. (1988), comparing CPP patients with normal controls, found that the CPP patients were significantly more likely to have a history of drug abuse or dependence. Reiter and Gambone (1990) found that CPP patients consume more medications than controls. These findings, taken together with the literature relating substance use to poor outcome of spine surgery, suggest that narcotic or alcohol dependence should be considered a risk factor for poor outcome of hysterectomy in CPP.

Sexual and Physical Abuse.   By far the largest body of research on psychological factors in CPP focuses on a history of sexual and physical abuse. Walker et al. (1988) found that CPP patients were victims of sexual abuse, both as a child and as an adult, much more frequently than were the normal controls. In fact, 64% of CPP patients had been sexual abuse victims before age 14. Reiter and Gambone (1990) also found that CPP patients were likely to have a history of sexual molestation. Similarly, Gross, Doerr, Caldirola, Guzinski, and Ripley (1980) found a high incidence of incest among CPP patients.

Rapkin, Kames, Darke, Sampler, and Naliboff (1990) compared CPP patients to patients having chronic pain in other locations, as well as to a nonpain control group. The CPP patients were much more likely than either of the other two groups to have experienced both childhood physical and sexual abuse. Interestingly, in this study CPP patients with no identifiable pathology were more likely to have experienced physical abuse rather than sexual abuse.

Once again, the incidence of sexual and physical abuse history among CPP patients is similar to that of spine pain patients. As noted in chapter 4, particularly in the research of Schofferman et al. (1992), abuse is both common among chronic back pain and is associated with diminished surgical results. Given its frequent incidence in the history of CPP patients, abuse should be carefully examined and considered a risk factor for poor outcome.

Marital and Couple Difficulties.   Because many patients with CPP have a history of physical and sexual abuse it is perhaps not surprising that marital dissatisfaction and upheaval are also quite common. As early as

1952, Duncan and Tyalor noted that marital dissatisfaction was common among patients with chronic "pelvic congestion." Gidro-Frank, Gordon, and Taylor (1980) interviewed patients with CPP and compared them to a group of prenatal women. Women in the CPP group were much more likely to be "critical" of their husbands, and toward their homes. Similar results were obtained by Renaer, Vertommen, Nijs, Wagemams, and van Hemel-rijck (1979).

There are a number of explanations for this high level of marital and relationship dissatisfaction among CPP patients. Certainly, these patients are likely to have sexual difficulties, including dyspareunia (painful inter-course), inhibited orgasm and inhibited sexual desire (E. Walker et al., 1988). Furthermore, as many of these patients have an abuse history, their communication skills and level of intimacy as adults may be adversely affected. For these and many other reasons, the CPP patient may lack the kind of stable and supportive relationship that can act as a "buffer" against stress and medical illness. Thus, just as with back pain, marital or relation-ship distress should be considered a common risk factor among CPP patients.

Personality Factors

As was noted in chapter 4, long-standing personality traits, as well as more current emotional states, can be assessed by objective psychometric testing. The major testing results that have been obtained in CPP follow here.

MMPI.   The MMPI has been used to investigate characteristics of patients with CPP. Renaer et al. (1979) used the MMPI to compare person-ality characteristics of CPP patients having no identifiable pathology with CPP patients diagnosed as having endometriosis, and with a control group. Both pain groups differed greatly from controls, showing elevations on scales *Hs, D,* and *Hy* of the MMPI. The pain groups also appeared to differ from the nonpain controls on scales *Pt* and *Si,* although the scores of the pain groups were not particularly elevated (*T* scores in the range of 50–60). The authors report that there was no major difference in MMPI profiles between the two pain groups. Based on these results, the authors concluded that that CPP patients without organic pathology do not differ from the endometriosis patients in "psychic functioning." Unfortunately, the study by Renaer suffers two major methodological flaws: (a) no statistical tests for group differences were reported; and (b) the number of subjects was quite small. For example, there were only 15 patients in the no organic pathology group. Thus, the main valid conclusion that can be drawn from this study is that patients with pelvic pain, regardless of cause, show elevations on scales *Hs, D,* and *Hy,* similar to those displayed by chronic back pain patients (see chapter 5).

Wood, Wood, and Reiter (1990) gave the MMPI to 81 women having CPP with negative laparoscopy results who were referred to a pelvic pain clinic. In this study, the authors compared the patients who reported a history of previous sexual trauma to patients reporting no past sexual trauma, and to those who did not respond to the sexual trauma history question. The CPP women from the trauma group showed a "V-type" MMPI pattern of elevations on scales *Hs* and *Hy,* with lower elevations on scale *D.* This same V-type MMPI pattern was also obtained by Gross et al. (1980) in a study of CPP patients with normal pelvic exams.

The results of MMPI research on CPP patients, although not strong, point in several familiar directions. Patients with CPP, perhaps especially those with negative laparoscopy results, show the elevations on scales *Hs* and *Hy.* These elevations, it will be remembered, are associated with two major characteristics: a high level of pain sensitivity; and a tendency to deny psychological problems while seeking medical explanation for the pain. In the case of CPP patients, these elevations seem especially to be associated with a history of sexual trauma. It may be that, of the many unfortunate consequences of sexual abuse, one is a tendency toward sensitivity to somatic problems. For example, Briere and Runtz (1988), examining adult survivors of childhood sexual abuse, found that these woman reported high levels of somatization, depression, and anxiety compared to a non-abused control group. Gross et al. (1980) found both a high level of somatization and a frequent history of incest among CPP patients having negative laparoscopy results. Whether or not pain sensitivity results from sexual abuse, *Hs* and *Hy* elevations are common among CPP patients and should be considered a strong risk factor for poor surgical outcome.

Depression.   Psychometric research on CPP patients also frequently uncovers evidence of clinical depression. Nolan, Methany, and Smith (1992), using the Beck Depression Inventory (BDI; Beck, Ward, Mendelsohn, Mock, & Erbaugh, 1961) found that 51% of CPP patients with negative laparoscopy results were clinically depressed. Interestingly, 72% of this patient population also reported significant sleep disturbance. Magni, Andreoli, de Leo, Martinotti, and Rossi (1986) found that negative laparoscopy CPP patients had higher depression levels on the Zung (1965) Depression Scale than did CPP patients with organic pathology and than normals. These authors concluded that "idiopathic pelvic pain could be a symptom of depression" (p. 168). Finally, E. Walker et al. (1988) found that CPP patients had higher scores on the depression scale of the SCL-90 than controls. These authors also found on interview that the CPP patients had a greater lifetime frequency of depressive episodes than did control patients.

As was noted in chapter 5, depression can sometimes be associated with poor outcome of back surgery. This is particularly true when the depression is chronic (i.e., it predates the back injury). Such chronically depressed patients may lack the ability to perceive positive events and may instead focus on somatic difficulties. Chronically depressed CPP patients are probably also less likely to achieve pain relief from hysterectomy. Acute clinical depression in CPP patients should be treated prior to undertaking any elective invasive procedure.

Summary

Patients with CPP share many characteristics with chronic back pain patients. In both patient groups there is a trend toward high levels of preexisting psychological problems and distress. There is also a high incidence rate of physical and sexual abuse in these populations. They tend to have a history of multiple physical symptoms in many body areas. They both tend to have high levels of marital distress and may overuse medications. Psychological testing may reveal tendencies toward excessive pain sensitivity and "disease conviction." Chronic depression is also frequently found. These results suggest that hysterectomy provided for the primary purpose of pain relief in CPP may likely be unsuccessful to the extent that the patient has a high level of psychological risk factors.

Temporomandibular Joint Dysfunction

TMD is a set of chronic pain conditions associated with symptoms in the masticatory and related muscles of the head and neck, and the soft tissue and bony components of the temporomandibular joint (TMJ; Dworkin & LeResche, 1992). The most common of these symptoms are reduced range of motion in the jaw, "clicking or popping" sounds in the TMJ , muscle spasms in the masseter region, pain in the periauriclar area (ear pain), and headache.

TMD problems are very common. Epidemiological research has shown that approximately 75% of the general population have at least one sign of

TMD, such as jaw movement abnormality, joint noise, or tenderness on palpation. Approximately one third of the population has at least one TMD symptom, such as face or joint pain (Rugh & Solberg, 1985; Schiffman, Fricton, Haley, & Shapiro, 1989). Von Korff et al. (1990), found a somewhat lower incidence rate, reporting that in a 6-month period, approximately 12% of an HMO population reported symptoms associated with TMD. Fortunately, it is estimated only 5% to 7% of individuals suffering TMD symptoms require further treatment (Randolph, Greene, Moretti, Forbes, & Perry, 1990; Rugh & Solberg, 1985).

TMD has long been recognized to be a complex phenomenon. Many pathophysiological conditions can give rise to these symptoms (Dworkin & LeResch, 1992), including, but not limited to:

- Muscle disorders, such as myofascial pain
- Displacement of the disc in the TMJ
- Degenerative conditions, such as osteoarthritis in the TMJ
- Pain arising from the joint capsule (arthralgia)

Because of this complexity, the treatments for TMD are quite varied. Some of the medical treatments include:

- Use of an orthopedic repositioning appliance ("bite plate") which maintains the mandible in a protruded position
- Trigger point injections, and stretch and spray techniques
- Grinding of the facets on the teeth to correct jaw position
- Anti-inflammatory medication and muscle relaxers
- Surgery to correct the TMJ problems

Most texts recognize that surgical approaches to TMD should only be undertaken as a last resort, after all other treatments have failed. In such protracted cases, aggressive repair of the joint may be the patient's only hope of pain relief. However, there is reason to believe that aggressive surgical intervention, even as a last ditch effort, may be problematic, for the TMD patient may have many of the same psychological problems displayed by other chronic pain patients.

It has long been acknowledged that the patient's psychological make-up plays a large role in TMD. This recognition was formalized in a report establishing research and diagnostic criteria in TMD (Dworkin & LeResche 1992). In this report, a dual axis approach was taken to TMD diagnosis. Axis I includes the patient's physical diagnosis, and Axis II includes "psychological distress and psychosocial dysfunction." By explicitly stating that TMD involves an interaction of physical and psychological factors, this report provides a strong rationale for the inclusion of PPS in the evaluation of TMD patients being considered for surgery. In this section, I review some of the psychological issues that have been observed among TMD patients.

Abuse History

A somewhat surprising finding among chronic pain patients is that many have a history of abuse. Such an unfortunate history also appears common in TMD. In a recent study, Curran et al. (1995), reviewing the history of 206 patients with orofacial pain, found that approximately 69% reported a history of physical or sexual abuse. Childhood physical abuse was twice as common (42%) as childhood sexual abuse (29%). Adult physical and sexual abuse was also quite prevalent. The authors also found that patients with a history of abuse had higher depression levels on the BDI, and higher overall psychological distress on the SCL-90. Furthermore, there was a significant correlation of abuse history with pain measures on the MPQ. The authors concluded that, "abused patients may feel unable to control their pain symptoms and may believe that their pain will persist. Such beliefs can exacerbate and/or prolong their facial pain symptoms" (p. 343).

Cognitive Factors: Expectancies and Explanatory Models

As with other pain syndromes, the ways in which the patient perceives and interprets the experience of the pain appear to play a large role in affecting TMD treatment outcome. Dworkin and associates at the University of Washington extensively investigated the role of such cognitive factors in TMD. Their investigations centered around patients' "explanatory models" for TMD (Dworkin et al., 1994; Massoth et al., 1994). In their research, *explanatory models* are defined as, "views, notions, beliefs and expectancies about an illness episode" (Kleinman, 1988).

A series of studies has investigated TMD patients' explanations of the relative roles played by physical factors, behaviors, and stress in causing, exacerbating, and maintaining TMD symptoms (Dworkin et al., 1994; Massoth et al., 1994). These studies demonstrate that patients who believe TMD is primarily caused by physical, as opposed to behavioral or stress-related factors, display a number of negative characteristics. First, patients with "physical" explanatory models have greater pain-related interference with daily activities. Second, they tend to use more passive pain-coping strategies, as assessed by the VPMI (G. Brown & Nicassio, 1987). Third, they tend to have greater levels of somatization, as assessed by the SCL-90 (Derogatis, 1983). Finally, patients who hold more physical explanatory models show greater restriction in mandibular range of motion than do patients with more behavioral or stress-related models.

Dworkin et al. (1994) conducted a study to determine whether brief psychoeducational group therapy could alter explanatory models and augment the results of conservative dental treatment for TMD. Results were compared between two groups of TMD patients: "dysfunctional" patients (who reported high levels of pain-related interference with daily activity) and "functional" patients (who reported lower levels of interference). Both at baseline and at two follow-up points, the dysfunctional patients showed reported greater pain, and had higher SCL-90 somatization scores, than did the functional patients, regardless of whether or not they were exposed to the group treatment. However, at no point did the two patient groups differ in an objective measure of TMD, unassisted jaw opening. In other words, the dysfunctional patients, whose lives were more disrupted by TMD symptoms, were able to open their mouths as well as the more functional patients. Thus, these results point to a familiar finding among chronic pain patients: Inconsistency between pain complaints and pain behaviors bode poorly for treatment outcome.

Personality Testing: MMPI.   Patients with TMD symptoms tend to have MMPI profiles that are similar to those seen in other chronic pain syndromes. R. Schwartz, Greene, and Laskin (1979) gave the MMPI to 42 TMD patients undergoing conservative treatment that included bite plates, physical therapy, and exercises. Patients who did not respond to the treatment had greater elevations on scales *Hy, Hs, D, Pd, Pt,* and *Sc* than did responsive patients. Millstein-Prentky and Olson (1979) found very similar results among 74 patients undergoing conservative TMD treatment. Again, unresponsive patients showed a tendency toward excessive pain sensitivity (as seen in elevated *Hy* and *Hs* scores), and agitated depression (as seen in elevated *D, Pd, Pt,* and *Sc* scores).

McCreary, Clark, Merril, and Oakley (1991) examined MMPI profiles of three groups of patients experiencing TMD: patients with "myalgia" (pain of diagnosed muscular origin), pain associated with TM joint problems (such as internal derangement or osteoarthritis), and a group with pain arising from both muscle and joint problems. The mylagia patients displayed the same type of profiles frequently encountered in chronic pain: Elevated scores were obtained on the *Hs, Hy, D,* and *Pt* scales. The scores for the myalgia patients were significantly higher on these scales than were the scores of the other two groups. The myalgia patients also showed significantly higher scores than the other TMD groups on the BDI, and on measures of anxiety. The authors concluded:

> (myalgia) patients showed higher scores on measures of concern about bodily function and preoccupation with illness. ... When myalgia patients are in pain and are preoccupied with worries about physical functioning and fearful about something going wrong with their body, they seem to be avoiding dealing with emotional aspects of their life. (p. 33)

Personality Testing: SCL-90. Somatization, as assessed by the SCL-90, is also associated with TMD problems. Dworkin et al. (1994) found that high somatization scores were associated with greater levels of pain-related interference in daily activities. Massoth et al. (1994) found somatization to be associated with "physical" explanatory models among TMD patients (see earlier). It would appear, then, that high somatization scores on the SCL-90, like high Hs and Hy scores on the MMPI, bode poorly for treatment outcome among patients with orofacial pain.

Summary

Once again, although the body of research on TMD is relatively small compared to back pain, a familiar pattern of findings is obtained. TMD patients have tendencies toward excessive pain complaints, as well as depression. A history of physical and sexual abuse is common. Those most dysfunctional TMD patients tend to hold beliefs that their symptoms are primarily physically based. Such beliefs may motivate them to seek surgery for pain relief, even though they may tend to have a higher level of psychological difficulties. Further, the dysfunctional patients show inconsistency between pain behavior and pain complaints: they are more disabled by pain despite having no greater objective limitations than the more functional patients.

General Model for PPS

As has been frequently noted throughout this text, surgical procedures are often considered for relief of chronic pain. In most chronic pain syndromes, such aggressive treatment approaches are only considered after more conservative measures, such as physical therapy, chiropractic, or injections, have failed to produce sufficient pain relief. Surgical procedures, then, become the culmination of a protracted, expensive, and frustrating set of experiences for the patient and physician alike.

Unfortunately, surgery often does not provide adequate relief of chronic pain. Even when the pain experience can be tied to damaged tissue, the surgery aimed at ameliorating this physical problem may do more harm than good. Surgery may not only fail to relieve pain, but also may lead to iatrogenic problems, such as scar tissue development, failure of implanted surgical hardware, or nerve damage. The chronic pain patient who is not helped by surgery is hastened along on a downward spiral of decreasing functional ability, worsening emotional state, and greater dependence on others and on the health care system.

The literature and information examined in this chapter, combined with the findings on back pain suggest that patients with disparate chronic pain syndromes share many common psychological characteristics. Some of these factors appear to militate against patients achieving relief of chronic pain as a result of surgery. This is not to say that surgery should never be undertaken for pain relief in chronic pain syndromes. Rather, it is suggested that PPS may provide an valuable tool for selecting those chronic pain patients unlikely to obtain good surgical results. Including PPS as part of a routine surgical work-up in this difficult patient population may, therefore, serve to enhance overall treatment results.

PPS procedures have not been thoroughly developed in many chronic pain syndromes. The information included in this practice guide, however, suggests some general guidelines for PPS, which are summarized in Fig. 8.1.

PPS Involves Examining Both Medical and Psychological Risk Factors

The behavioral health practitioner performing the PPS needs to understand both the medical conditions and psychological factors associated with the particular chronic pain syndrome being investigated. A thorough review of the medical records should be a part of the PPS. In addition, the referring surgeon may need to be questioned in order to understand the proposed surgery, its rationale and expected effects. The behavioral health practitioner then should perform a semistructured psychological interview and provide appropriate psychological testing, in order to determine the level of psychological risk for poor outcome.

Level of Medical Risk Should Be Ascertained

Medical risk factors exist in the situations as discussed here.

Name: _____   Onset: _____   Date: _____
Med Dx: _____   Surg. Type: _____   ID: _____
MD: _____   Psych: _____

Medical Risk	**Psych Risk**	**Judgment Factors**
Unclear Pathology __	Disincentives __	Non-Compliance __
Unclear Pain-Pathology Relationship __	Upheaval __	Negative Attitude __
	Long-Term Psych __	Poor Prev. Recover __
Low Efficacy __	Abuse __	Maladaptive __
Hi Iatrogenic __	Inconsistency __	Other: _____ __
Long Recovery __	Drugs or ETOH __	_____ __
Pain > 1 yr. __	Pain Sensitivity __	
Prev. Medical __	Cognitive Factors __	
Prev. Surgery __		
Med Total __	Psych Total __	
Threshold = 4 ± 1	Threshold = 4 ± 1	
MED RISK = ___	PSYCH RISK = ___	

PROGNOSIS	MED TREATMENT RECOMMENDATIONS
GOOD	Clear for surgery, no psych necessary
	Clear for surgery, post-op psych
FAIR	Hold, pending psych intervention
	Do not operate, conservative care only
POOR	Do not operate, recommend discharge

FIG. 8.1.   General PPS.

Pathophysiological Condition Underlying the Pain is Not Clearly Identified.   In some pain syndromes, such as CPP, no pathology can be discerned. In most pain syndromes, the identification of pathology is not dichotomous. Different levels of the same type of pathology may be encountered. For example, lumbar disc herniation may be minimal, moderate, or severe (see chapter 3). Similarly, the level of endometriosis identified laparoscopically in CPP may be quite variable. A medical risk factor for poor outcome is identified to the extent that the pathophysiology associated with the pain is minimal.

Relationship Between the Identified Pathophysiology and Pain is Not Clearly Demonstrated. Just demonstrating that the chronic pain patient has abnormal test results does not mean that the identified pathology is the source of pain. As noted in chapter 3, many individuals with no back pain have abnormal-appearing discs on MRI. Medical testing should link the pathology to the pain experience, either by techniques that briefly exacerbate the pain (such as palpation, or pressure) or ablate the nociception arising from the pathology (perhaps through anesthetic injection, TENS units, etc.).

Low Demonstrated Efficacy of the Surgical Intervention for Providing Pain Relief. Most surgeries for the relief of chronic pain have been investigated scientifically. It is suggested that less than 80% probability of pain relief from surgery constitutes a medical risk factor for poor outcome.

High Probability of Developing Iatrogenic Physical Problems. The probability of surgical failure and the development of additional postoperative medical problems have been investigated in connection with most surgeries. This risk factor is identified if the surgery is associated with a 10% or greater chance of developing new medical problems as a result of the surgery. Generally, the more "destructive" the surgery, the higher the probability of iatrogenic difficulties.

Lengthy Recovery Time From Surgery. Lengthy recovery time allows for the development of intense emotional difficulties, pain behaviors and medication dependence. It is suggested that the procedure is associated with high risk if the recovery time is predicted to be greater than 2 months.

Patient Has Experienced Pain for More Than 1 Year. With increasing chronicity comes the opportunity for the development of more firmly entrenched pain behaviors. After 1 year, the probability of good treatment outcome is significantly diminished.

Patient Has Been Treated for Numerous Other Medical Conditions. This factor is easily identified by determining the number of previous medical treatments and hospitalizations for conditions other than the one being treated at the time of the evaluation. Patients who tend to seek many physicians, and run up large medical bills, associated with an excessive number of physical symptoms, will likely respond poorly to pain-related surgery. This is especially true if the patient has been treated for other chronic pain syndromes in the past.

Patient Has Previously Received Surgery for Relief of Current Pain Condition.   The likelihood of good surgical outcome tends to diminish with successive surgeries. Previous failed surgery is a very strong predictor of poor outcome.

The patient should be considered to have a high level of medical risk if four or more of the situations just discussed are present.

Psychological Risk Factors Should Be Determined

Psychological risk factors are present in situations such as those discussed here.

Behavioral and Financial Disincentives to Recovery Exist.   Such features might include the receipt of worker's compensation payments, third-party litigation related to the pain, disability payments, and job dissatisfaction. Also included in this category is reinforcement by the spouse or family of disability. These factors may make the punishment for recovery from the pain greater than the rewards.

Patient's Current Psychosocial Situation is Characterized by Upheaval and Distress.   These factors include expressed marital distress, dissatisfaction or recent divorce, distressing social isolation, or a high level of problems with friends and family. These factors may make it difficult for the patient to focus energy on recovery from surgery.

Patient Has History of Long-Standing Emotional Difficulties.   Patients may have a history of psychiatric hospitalizations or lengthy outpatient treatments. Many patients may report a history of intense psychological problems, but without ever having sought treatment. The patient with a long history of psychological difficulties may be ill-equipped to deal with the stresses involved in surgery and recovery. For patients who are depressed or experience diagnosable mental health problems in reaction to an injury or disease condition, the psychological problem is only a risk factor to the extent that it is not appropriated treated.

Patient Has Been a Victim of Abuse or Abandonment. This factor is primarily identified by patient reports of early or current victimization. Certainly, current abuse is more problematic than a past history of such problems, but both seem to bode poorly for treatment outcome.

Inconsistency Between Patient's Pain Behavior and Pain Reports. I n most pain syndromes "normal" pain behaviors have been described. Pain has a normal distribution throughout the body in each syndrome. Certain activities and diagnostic techniques, such as palpation, should elicit particular types of pain responses. This risk factor is identified to the extent that the patient's pain reports are not consistent with the level of pain behavior displayed, or are inconsistent with "normal" complaints in the particular pain syndrome.

Patient Abuses Narcotic Medications or Alcohol. Abuse of prescription medication is easily identified through chart review and discussion with the physician. High levels of narcotic consumption, if prescribed by the physician, are not necessarily a risk factor. Rather, it is drug-seeking behavior (see chapter 4) that bodes poorly for surgery. Patients who call in early for prescription refills or fabricate excuses for losing narcotics should be suspect. Abuse of street drugs and alcohol is more difficult to identify, short of directly observing signs of intoxication. If the behavioral health practitioner suspects this problem the patient should be asked to submit to random serum alcohol and drug testing.

Patient Has Tendency Toward Excessive Pain Sensitivity or Excessive Physical Complaints. Perhaps the most consistent predictor of poor surgical outcome, cutting across all chronic pain syndromes, can be characterized as excessive pain sensitivity. MMPI scale elevations, particularly on Hs and Hy, are useful for identifying this risk factor. The somatization scale of the SCL-90 may also be useful.

Patient Perceives Little Influence Over Course of Pain and Expects Physician to Provide Pain Relief. Cognitive questionnaires, such as the CSQ or the VMPI, can identify patients who tend to catastrophize, and to externalize responsibility for cure. Both of these factors indicate a patient with little motivation for the rehabilitation efforts and pain tolerance required in recovering from surgery for chronic pain.

The patient should be considered to have a high level of psychological risk if four or more of the situations just discussed are present.

Overall Surgical Prognosis Should Be Determined From the Combined Medical and Psychological Risk Factors

Surgical prognosis follows from identification of medical and psychological risk factors. Prognosis can be determined using the model developed in chapter 6 (see Fig. 8.2). If the patient has both low medical and psychological risk, good surgical prognosis is determined. Fair prognosis occurs when the patient has a high level of risk on one dimension and a low level of risk on the other. Poor prognosis results when both risk levels are high.

Clinical judgment can be exercised when the client's number of risk factors is near threshold level. Such judgment can be used when the patient displays three to five of the medical risk factors just listed, or when the patient displays three to five of the psychological risk factors just listed. When using clinical judgment, the patient is moved from one side of the high-risk threshold to the other. Thus, the decision about surgical prognosis can be altered, based on factors observed during the PPS, but not specifically listed previously. However, because clinical judgment can only be applied when patients fall into a narrow range of risk factors, the use of this technique basically ties the decision on surgical prognosis to specific criteria, while permitting the practitioner some clinical latitude. As noted

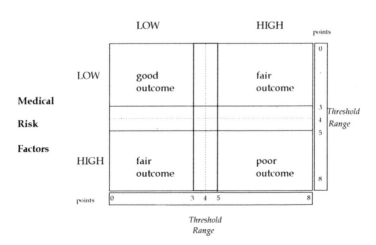

FIG. 8.2. General surgery prognosis determined by medical and psychological risk factors.

in chapter 6, some of the factors that might cause the practitioner to move the threshold include:

- History of noncompliance
- Ambivalent or negative attitude toward physician and surgery
- History of having recovered poorly (or well) from previous pain-related surgery, etc.
- Maladaptive behaviors such as "extortion" or "staff splitting"

Psychological Treatment Plans Should Be Developed

As has been noted frequently throughout this text, PPS does not end when the decision on surgical prognosis is determined. Rather the behavioral health practitioner is then presented with the opportunity to assist in the patient's recovery and bring the case to a conclusion. Treatment plans should generally be directed toward the following goals:

- Improving motivation and compliance
- Developing pain control and coping strategies
- Reducing dependence on narcotics and alcohol
- Involving family and significant others in recovery
- Using community resources, such as vocational rehabilitation counselors, library research, etc., to assist in rehabilitation
- Developing realistic outcome expectancies and sense of responsibility for improvement

More specific types of treatment recommendations are related to the patient's surgical prognosis, as listed in chapter 6.

Summary and Conclusion

Surgery is not infrequently considered for relief of pain in a wide variety of chronic pain syndromes. Before such surgery is undertaken, PPS should be seriously considered. Patients with widely varying chronic pain syndromes share a number of common psychological characteristics, many of which may negatively influence surgical outcome. For example, the most treatment-resistant patients tend to have a high level of pain sensitivity, as well as a history of multiple physical complaints. Depression is also common, and may sometimes predate the pain-producing injury. Other long-term psychological and psychiatric difficulties are frequent. Marital and vocational upheaval are common among recalcitrant pain patients. Drug and alcohol abuse may also be seen. There is also a surprisingly high number of treatment-resistant patients who have experienced physical and/or sexual abuse. PPS can identify the presence of these and other risk factors, and determine whether, overall, the patient is likely to experience pain relief as a result of surgery.

PPS is a scientifically valid procedure that is, at once, humanitarian and cost-effective, providing a significant service to the patient, the physician, and the insurance community. PPS can help potentially unresponsive patients avoid the months or years of additional pain and medical treatment that can follow from failed surgery. PPS can augment the surgical results obtained, even for patients who are good risks. For the physician, it can improve overall treatment outcome, and help avoid "problem patients." By screening out inappropriate surgical candidates, PPS can save a great deal of money for insurance companies. Thus, through careful applications of PPS, the behavioral health practitioner can provide invaluable insight into the effective treatment of the chronic pain patient.

References

American Psychiatric Association. (1987). *Diagnostic and statistical manual of mental disorders* (3rd ed., rev.). Washington, DC: Author.

American Psychiatric Association. (1994). *Diagnostic and statistical manual of mental disorders* (4th ed.). Washington DC: Author.

An, H. S., Silveri, C. P., Simpson, M., File, P., Simmons, C., Simeone, A., & Balderston, R. A. (1994). Comparison of smoking habits between patients with surgically confirmed herniated lumbar and cervical disc disease and controls. *Journal of Spinal Disorders, 7*(5), 369–373.

Anastasi, A. (1994). *Psychological testing.* New York: Macmillan.

Atkinson, J. H. (1989). Psychopharmacologic agents in the treatment of pain syndromes. In C. D. Tollison (Ed.), *Handbook of chronic pain management* (pp. 69–103). Baltimore: Williams & Wilkins.

Baker, P. N., & Symonds, E. M. (1992). The resolution of chronic pelvic pain after normal laparoscopy findings. *American Journal of Obstetrics and Gynecology, 166,* 835–836.

Bandura, A. (1977). Self-efficacy: Toward a unifying theory of behavioral change. *Psychological Review, 37,* 747–755.

Barber, J., & Adrian, C. (Eds.). (1985). *Psychological approaches to the management of pain.* New York: Brunner/Mazel.

Barnes, D., Smith, D., Gatchel, R. J., & Mayer, T. G. (1989). Psychosocioeconomic predictors of treatment success/failure in chronic low back patients. *Spine, 14,* 427–430.

Barron, M., & Zazandijan, V. A. (1993). Geographic variation in lumbar discectomy: A protocol for evaluation. *QBR, 18,* 98–197.

Basmajian, J. V. (1983). *Biofeedback: Principles and practice for clinicians* (2nd ed.). Baltimore: Williams & Wilkins.

Baumstark, K. F., Buckelew, S. P., Sher, K. J., Beck, N., Buescher, K. L., Hewett, J., & Crews, T. M. (1993). Pain behavior predictors among fibromyalgia patients, *Pain, 55,* 339–346.

Beck, A. T., Ward, C. H., Mendelsohn, M., Mock, J., & Erbaugh, J. (1961). An inventory for measuring depression. *Archives of General Psychiatry, 4,* 561–571.

Bigos, S. J., Battie, M. C., Spengler, D. M., Fisher, L. D., Fordyce, W. E., Hansson, T., Nachemson, A. L., & Worthly, M. D. (1991). A prospective study of work perceptions and psychosocial factors affecting the report of back injury. *Spine, 16,* 1–6.

Blitz, B., & Dinnerstein, A. J. (1971). Role of attentional focus in pain perception: Manipulation of response to noxious stimulation by instructions. *Journal of Abnormal Psychology*, 77(1), 42–45.

Block, A. R. (1981). An investigation of the response of the spouse to chronic pain behavior. *Psychosomatic medicine*, 43(5), 415–422.

Block, A. R. (1982). Multidisciplinary treatment of chronic low back pain: A review. *Rehabilitation Psychology*, 27, 51–63.

Block, A. R. (1992). Psychological screening of spine surgery candidates. In S. H. Hochschuler, H. B. Cotler, & R. D. Guyer (Eds.), *Rehabilitation of the spine: Science and practice* (pp. 617–625). St. Louis: Mosby.

Block, A. R., & Boyer, S. L. (1984). The spouse's adjustment to chronic pain: Cognitive and emotional factors. *Social Science Medicine*, 19, 1313–1317.

Block, A. R., Boyer, S. L., & Silbert, R. V. (1985). Spouse's perception of the chronic pain patient: Estimates of exercise tolerance. In H. L. Fields, R. Dubner, & F. Cervero (Eds.), *Advances in pain research and therapy* (Vol 9, pp. 897–904). New York: Raven Press.

Block, A. R., Kremer, E. F., & Gaylor, M. (1980a). Behavioral treatment of chronic pain: The spouse as a discriminative cue for pain behavior. *Pain*, 9, 243–252.

Block, A. R., Kremer, E. F., & Gaylor, M. (1980b). Behavioral treatment of chronic pain: Variables affecting treatment efficacy. *Pain*, 8, 367–375.

Block, A. R., Vanharanta, H., Ohnmeiss, D., & Guyer, R. D. (1996). Discographic pain report: Influence of psychological factors. *Spine*, 21 , 334–338.

Bonica, J. J. (Ed.). (1990). *The management of pain* (2nd ed.). Philadelphia: Lea & Febiger.

Bradley, L. A., Prokop, C. K., Gentry, W. D., Van der Heide, L. H., & Prieto, E. J. (1981). Assessment of chronic pain. In C. K. Prokop & L. A. Bradley (Eds.), *Medical psychology: Contributions to behavioral medicine* (pp. 91–91). New York: Academic Press.

Breuer, J., & Freud, S. (1895). *Studies in hysteria.* New York: Basic Books.

Briere, J., & Runtz, M. (1988). Symptomatology associated with childhood sexual victimization in a nonclinical adult sample. *Child Abuse and Neglect*, 12, 51–59.

Brown, C. W., Orme, T. J., & Richardson, H. D. (1986). The rate of pseudoarthrosis (surgical non-union) in patients who are smokers and patients who are nonsmokers: A comparison study. *Spine*, 2, 942.

Brown, G. K., & Nicassio, P. M. (1987). Development of a questionnaire for the assessment of active and passive coping strategies in chronic pain patients. *Pain*, 31, 53–64.

Buckelew, S. P., Parker, J. C., Keefe, J. F., Deuser, W. E., Crews, T. M., Conway, R., Kay, D. R., & Hewett, J. E. (1994). Self-efficacy and pain behavior among subjects with fibromyalgia. *Pain*, 59, 377–384.

Butcher, J. N. (1990). *The MMPI-2 in psychological treatment.* New York: Oxford University Press.

Cairns, D., & Pasino, J. A. (1977). Comparison of verbal reinforcement and feedback in the operant treatment of disability due to chronic low back pain. *Behavior Therapy*, 8, 621–630.

Carlson, C. R., Okeson, J. P., Falace, D. A., Nitz, A. J., Curran. S. L., & Anderson, D. (1993). Comparison of psychologic and physiologic functioning between patients with masticatory muscle pain and matched controls. *Journal of Orofacial Pain*, 7, 15–22.

Cashion, E. L., & Lynch, W. J. (1979). Personality factors and results of lumbar disc surgery. *Neurosurgery 4,* 141–145.

Cattell, R. B., Eber, H. W., & Tatsuoka, M. M. (1970). *Handbook for the Sixteen Personality Factor Questionnaire.* Champaign, IL: Institute for Personality and Ability Testing.

Cavanaugh, S., Clark, D. C., & Gibbons, R. D. (1983). Diagnosing depression in the hospitalized medically ill. *Psychosomatics, 24,* 809–815.

Chapman, R. C. (1978). Pain: The perception of noxious events. In R. A. Sternbach (Ed.), *The psychology of pain* (pp. 169–202). New York: Raven Press.

Cinciripini, P. M., Lapitsky, L., Seay, S., Wallfisch, A., Kitchens, K., & Van Vunakis, H. (1995). The effects of smoking schedules on cessation outcome: Can we improve on common methods of gradual and abrupt nicotine withdrawal? *Journal of Consulting and Clinical Psychology, 63*(3), 388–399.

Ciol, M. A., Deyo, R. A., Kreuter, W., & Bigos, S. J. (1994). Characteristics in medicare beneficiaries associated with reoperation after lumbar spine surgery. *Spine, 19*(12), 1329–1334.

Coste, J., Paolaggi, J. B., & Spira, A. (1992a). Classification of nonspecific low back pain. II. Clinical diversity of organic forms. *Spine, 17*(9), 1038–1042.

Coste, J., Paolaggi, J. B., & Spira, A. (1992b). Classification of nonspecific low back pain. I. Psychological involvement in low back pain: A clinical, descriptive approach. *Spine, 17*(9), 1028–1037.

Curran, S. L., Sherman, J. J., Cunningham, L. C., Okeson, J. P., Reid, K. K., & Carlson, C. R. (1995). Physical and sexual abuse among orofacial pain patients: Linkages with pain and psychologic distress. *Journal of Orofacial Pain, 9*(4), 340–345.

Cypress, B. K. (1983). Characteristics of physician visits for back symptoms: A nominal perspective. *American Journal of Public Health, 73,* 389–395.

Davis, R. A. (1994). A long-term outcome analysis of 984 surgically treated herniated lumbar discs. *Journal of Neurosurgery, 80,* 514–421.

DeGood, D. E., & Kiernan, B. (1996). Perception of fault in patient with chronic pain. *Pain, 64,* 153–159

Derogatis, L. R. (1977). *SCL-90R.* Towson, MD: Clinical Psychometric Research.

Derogatis, L. R. (1983). *SCL-90-R: Administration, scoring and procedures manual—II for the revised version.* Towson, MD: Clinical Psychometric Research. Deyo, R. A., & Diehl, A. K. (1988). Psychosocial predictors of disability in patients with low back pain. *The Journal of Rheumatology, 15*(10), 1557–1564.

Deyo, R. A., Diehl, A., & Rosenthan, M. (1986). How many days of bedrest for acute low back pain? *New England Journal of Medicine, 315,* 1064–1070.

Dolce J. J., Crocker, M. F., & Doleys, D. M. (1986). Prediction of outcome among chronic pain patients. *Behavioral Research Therapy, 14,* 313–319.

Dolce, J. J., Crocker, M. F., Moletteire, C., & Doleys, D. M. (1986). Exercise quotas, anticipatory concern and self-efficacy expectancies in chronic pain: A preliminary report. *Pain, 24,* 365–372.

Doxey, N. C., Dzioba, R. B., & Mitson, G. L. (1988). Predictors of outcome in back surgery candidates. *Journal of Clinical Psychology, 44,* 611–622.

Drossman, D. A., Leserman, J., Nachman, G., Zhiming, L., Gluck, H., Toomey, T. C., & Mitchell, C. M. (1990). Sexual and physical abuse in women with functional or organic gastrointestinal disorders. *Annals of Internal Medicine, 113,* 828–833.

Duncan, C. H., & Taylor, H. D. (1952). Psychosomatic study of pelvic congestion. *American Journal of Obstetrics and Gynecology, 64,* 1–6.

Dvorak, J., Valach, L., Fuhrimann, P., & Heim, E. (1988). The outcome of surgery for lumbar disc herniation. II. A 4–17 years' follow-up with emphasis on psychosocial aspects. *Spine, 13*(12), 1423–1427.

Dworkin, S. F., & LeResche, L. (1992). Research diagnostic criteria for Temporomandibular Disorders. *Journal of Craniomandibular Disorders and Facial Oral Pain, 6,* 3–11.

Dworkin, S. F., Turner, J. A., Wilson, L., Massoth, D., Whitney, C., Huggins, K. H., Burgess, J., Sommers, E., & Truelove, E. (1994). Brief group cognitive–behavioral intervention for temporomandibular disorders. *Pain, 59,* 175–187.

Dzioba, R. B., & Doxey, N. C. (1984). A prospective investigation in the orthopedic and psychologic predictors of outcome of first lumbar surgery following industrial injury. *Spine, 9,* 614–623.

Eccleston, C. (1995). The attentional control of pain: Methodological and theoretical concerns. *Pain, 63,* 400–402.

Eker, J. P., & Wiseman, L. W. (1994, December). Medical review guidelines for lumbar spinal surgery. *Private Healthcare Systems Review,* 2–4.

Elkins, G. R., & Barrett, E. T. (1984). The MMPI in evaluation of functional versus organic low back pain. *Journal of Personality Assessment, 48,* 259–264.

Ellis, A. (1962). *Reason and emotion in psychotherapy.* New York: Lyle Stuart.

Engle, G. L. (1959). "Psychogenic" pain and the pain-prone patient. *American Journal of Medicine, 26,* 899–918.

Estlander, A. M. (1989). Coping strategies in low back pain: Effects of severity of pain, situation, gender, and duration of pain. *Scandinavian Journal of Behavior Therapy, 18,* 20–29.

Estlander, A. M., Vanharanta, H., Moneta, G. B., & Kavinto, K. (1994). Anthropometric variables, self-efficacy beliefs, and pain and disability ratings on the isokinetic performance of low back pain patients. *Spine, 19*(8), 941–947.

Fairbank, J. C. T., Couper, J., Davies, J., & O'Brien, J. P. (1980). The Oswestry low back pain disability questionnaire. *Physiotherapy, 66,* 271–273.

Fernandez, E., & Turk, D. C. (1989). The utility of coping strategies for altering pain perception: A meta-analysis. *Pain, 38*(2), 123–135.

Fernandez, E., & Turk, D. C. (1995). The scope and significance of anger in the experience of chronic pain. *Pain, 61,*165–175.

Fields, H. L. (Ed.). (1991). *Core curriculum for professional education in pain.* Seattle: IASP Press.

Finneson, B. E., & Cooper, V. R. (1979). A lumbar disc surgery predictive score card: A retrospective evaluation. *Sine, 4,* 141–144.

Fishbain, D. A., Goldberg, M., Meagher, B. R., Steele, R., & Rosomoff, H. (1986). Male and female chronic pain patients categorized by DSM–III psychiatric diagnostic criteria. *Pain, 26,* 181–197.

Flor, H., Fydrich, T., & Turk, D. C. (1992). Efficacy of multidisciplinary pain treatment centers: A meta-analytic review. *Pain, 49,* 221–230.

Folkman S., & Lazarus, R. S. (1985). An analysis of coping in a middle aged community sample. *Journal of Health and Social Behavior, 21,* 219–239.

Fordyce, W. E. (1976). *Behavioral methods for chronic pain and illness.* St. Louis: Mosby.

Fordyce, W. E. (1978). Learning process in pain. In R. A. Sternbach (Ed.), *The Psychology of pain.* New York: Raven Press.

Fordyce, W. E., Brena, S. F., Holcomb, R. J., De Lauteur, B. J., & Loeser, J. (1978). Relationship of patient semantic pain descriptions to physician diagnostic judgments, activity level measures and MMPI. *Pain, 5* (3), 293–303.

Fordyce, W. E., Brockway, J. A., & Spengler, D. (1986). Acute back pain: A control group comparison of behavioral versus traditional management models. *Journal of Behavioral Medicine, 4,* 127.

Franklin, G. M., Haug, J., Heyer, N. J., McKeefrey, S. P., & Picciano, J. F. (1994). Outcome of lumbar fusion in Washington State workers' compensation. *Spine, 19* (17), 1897–1904.

Freeman, C., Calsyn, D., & Loucks, J. (1976). The use the Minnesota Multiphasic Personality Inventory with low back pain patients. *Journal of Clinical Psychology, 32* (2), 294–298.

Frymoyer, J. W. (1991). *The adult spine: Principles and practice.* New York: Raven Press.

Frymoyer, J. W. (1993). Quality: An international challenge to the diagnosis and treatment of disorders of the lumbar spine. *Spine, 15,* 2147–2151.

Frymoyer, J. W., & Cats-Baril, W. L. (1987). An overview of the incidences and cost of low back pain. *Orthopedic Clinics of America, 22,* 263–271.

Frymoyer, J. W., Pope, H. J., Clements, J. H., Wilder, D. G., MacPherson, D., & Ashikagar, T. (1983). Risk factors in low back pain—an epidemiological survey. *Journal of Bone and Joint Surgery (America) 65,* 213–215.

Gamsa, A. (1994). The role of psychological factors in chronic pain. II. A critical appraisal. *Pain, 57,* 17–29.

Gatchel, R. J., Mayer, T. G., Capra, P., Barnett, J., & Diamond, P. (1986). Millon behavioral health inventory: Its utility in predicting physical function in patients with low back pain. *Archives of Physical Medical Rehabilitation, 67,* 878–882.

Gidro-Frank, L., Gordon, T., & Taylor, H. C. (1960). Pelvic pain and female identity. *American Journal of Obstetrics and Gynecology, 79,* 1184–1202.

Gil, K. M., Abrams, M. R., Phillips, G., & Keefe, F. J. (1990). Sickle cell disease pain: Relation of coping strategies to adjustment. *Journal of Consulting and Clinical Psychology, 57,* 725–731.

Graham, J. R. (1990). *The MMPI-2: Assessing personality and psychopathology.* New York: Oxford University Press.

Greenough, C. G., & Fraser, R. D. (1989). The effects of compensation on recovery from low-back injury. *Spine, 14*(9), 947–955.

Grimm, L., & Kanfer, F. H. (1976). Tolerance of aversive stimulation. *Behavior Therapy, 7,* 593–601.

Gross, A. R. (1986). The effect of coping strategies on the relief of pain following surgical intervention for lower back pain. *Psychosomatic Medicine, 48,* 229–238.

Gross, R. J., Doerr, H., Caldirola, D., Guzinski, G., & Ripley, H. S. (1980). Borderline syndrome and incest in chronic pain patients. *International Journal of Psychiatry in Medicine, 10,* 70–86.

Haber, J., & Roos, C. (1985). Effects of spouse abuse and/or sexual abuse in the development and maintenance of chronic pain in women. *Advances in Pain and Research Therapy, 9,* 889–895.

Haddad, G. H. (1987). Analysis of 2932 workers' compensation back injury cases: The impact of the cost to the system. *Spine, 12* (8), 765–271.

Hanvik, L. J. (1950). MMPI profiles in patients with low–back pain. *Journal of Consulting Psychology, 15,* 350–353.

Herron, L., Turner, J. A., Ersek, M., & Weiner, P. (1992). Does the Millon Behavioral Health Inventory (MBHI) predict lumbar laminectomy outcome? A comparison with the Minnesota Multiphasic Personality Inventory (MMPI). *Journal of Spinal Disorders, 5*(2), 188–192.

Hilgard, E. R. (1978). Hypnosis and pain. In R. A. Sternbach (Ed.), *The psychology of pain* (pp. 219–240). New York: Raven Press.

Hilgard, E. R., & Hilgard, J. R. (1975). *Hypnosis in the relief of pain.* Los Altos, CA: William Kaufman.

Hoffman, R. M., Wheeler, K. J., & Deyo, R. A. (1993). Surgery for herniated lumbar discs: A literature synthesis. *Journal of General Internal Medicine, 8,* 487–496.

Hudgins, W. R. (1976). Laminectomy for treatment of lumbar disc disease. *Texas Medicine, 72,* 65–69.

Hughes, J. R. (1993). Pharmacotherapy for smoking cessation: Unvalidated assumptions, anomalies, and suggestions for future research. *Journal of Consulting and Clinical Psychology, 81*(5), 751–760.

Jeffrey, R. W., Wing, R. R., Thorson, C., Burton, L. R., Raether, C., Harvey, J., & Mullen, M. (1993). Strengthening behavioral interventions for weight loss: A randomized trial of food provision and monetary incentives. *Journal of Consulting and Clinical Psychology, 61*(6), 1038–1045.

Jensen, M. P., & Karoly, P. (1991). Control beliefs, coping efforts, and adjustment to chronic pain. *Journal of Consulting and Clinical Psychology, 59,* 431–438.

Jensen, M. P., Karoly, P., & Huger, R. (1987). The development and preliminary validation of an instrument to assess patients' attitude toward pain. *Journal of Psychosomatic Research, 31,* 393–400.

Jensen, M. P., Turner, J. A., Romano, J. M. (1991). Self-efficacy and outcome expectancies: relationship to chronic pain coping strategies and adjustment. *Pain, 44,* 263–269.

Jensen, M. P., Turner, J. A., & Romano, J. M. (1994). Correlates of improvement in multidisciplinary treatment of chronic pain. *Journal of Consulting and Clinical Psychology, 62*(1), 172–179.

Jensen, M. P., Turner, J. A., Romano, J. M., & Karoly, P. (1991). Coping with chronic pain: A critical review of the literature. *Pain, 47,* 249–283.

Junge, A., Dvorak, J., & Ahrens, S. (1995). Predictors of bad and good outcomes of lumbar disc surgery: A prospective clinical study with recommendations for screening to avoid bad outcomes. *Spine, 20*(4), 460–468.

Keefe, F. J., & Block, A. R. (1982a). Biofeedback and behavioral medicine. In J. Caven & H. K. H. Brody (Eds.), *Critical problems in psychiatry 1982–1983.* New York: Academic Press.

Keefe, F. J., & Block, A. R. (1982b). Development of an observation method for assessing pain behavior in chronic low back pain patients. *Behavioral Therapy, 13,* 636–375.

Keefe, F. J., Brown, G. K., Wallston, K. A., & Caldwell, D. S. (1989). Coping with rheumatoid arthritis pain: Catastrophizing as a maladaptive strategy. *Pain, 37,* 51–56.

Keefe, F. J., Caldwell, D. S., Queen, K. T., Gil, K. M., Martinez, S., Crisson, J. E. Ogden, W., & Nunley, J. (1987). Pain coping strategies in osteoarthritis patients. *Journal of Consulting and Clinical Psychology, 55,* 208–212.

Keefe, F. J., Crisson, J., Urban, B. J., & Williams, D. A. (1990). Analyzing chronic low back pain: The relative contribution of pain coping strategies. *Pain, 40,* 293–301.

Keefe, F. J., & Dolan, E. (1986). Pain behavior and pain coping strategies in low back pain and myofascial pain dysfunction syndrome patients. *Pain, 24,* 49–56.

Keefe, F. J., Salley, A. N., & Lefevbre, J. C. (1992). Coping with pain: Conceptual concerns and future directions. *Pain, 51,* 131–134.

Keel, P. J. (1984). Psychosocial criteria for patient selection: Review of studies and concepts for understanding chronic back pain. *Neurosurgery, 15*(6), 935–941.

Keller, L. S., & Butcher, J. N. (1991). *Assessment of chronic pain patients with the MMPI-2 [MMPI-2 Monographs]* (Vol. 2.) Minneapolis: University of Minnesota Press.

Kennedy, F. (1946). The mind of the injured worker: Its affect on disability periods. *Compensation Medicine, 1,* 19–24.

Kerns, R. D., Turk, D. C., & Rudy, E. E. (1985). The West Haven–Yale Multidimensional Pain Inventory (WHYMPI). *Pain, 23,* 345–356.

Kinney, R. K., Gatchel, R. J., & Mayer, T. G. (1991). (The SCL-90R evaluated as an alternative to the MMPI for psychological screening of chronic low-back pain patients. *Spine, 16,* 940–942.

Kinney, R. K., Gatchel, R. J., Polatin, P. B., Fogarty, W. T., & Mayer, T. G. (1993). Prevalence of psychopathology in acute and chronic low back pain patients. *Journal of Occupational Rehabilitation, 3*(2), 95–103.

Kleinke, C. L., & Spangler, A. S. (1988a). Predicting treatment outcome of chronic back pain patients in a multidisciplinary pain clinic: Methodological issues and treatment implications. *Pain, 33,* 41–48.

Kleinke, C.L., & Spangler, A. D. (1988b). Psychometric analysis of the audiovisual taxonomy for assessing pain behavior in chronic back pain patients. *Journal of Behavioral Medicine, 11,* 83–94.

Kleinman, A. (1988). *The illness narratives: Suffering, healing and the human condition.* New York: Basic Books.

Kopec, J. A., & Esdaile, J. M. (1995). Functional disability scales for back pain. *Spine, 20,* 1943–1949.

Kremer, E. F., Block, A. R., & Atkinson, J. J. (1983). Assessment of pain behavior: Factors that distort self-report. In R. Melzack (Ed.), *Pain management and assessment* (pp. 165–171). New York: Raven Press.

Kresche, A. J., Seifer, D. B., Sachs, L. B., & Barrese, I. (1984). Laparoscopy in 100 women with chronic pelvic pain. *Obstetrics and Gynecology, 64,* 672–674.

Kuperman, S. K., Osmon, D., Golden, C. J., & Blume, I. (1979). Prediction of neurosurgical results by psychological evaluation. *Perceptual Motor Skills, 48,* 311–315.

Lankton, S. R., & Lankton, C. H. (1983). *The answer within: A clinical framework of Ericksonian hypnotherapy.* New York: Brunner/Mazel.

Lawson, K., Reesor, K. A., Keefe, F. J., & Turner, J. A. (1990). Dimensions of pain-related cognitive coping: Cross validation of the factor structure of the Coping Strategy Questionnaire. *Pain, 43,* 195–204.

Lazarus, R. A., & Folkman, S. (1984). *Appraisal and coping.* New York: Springer.

Leavitt, F., & Sweet, J. J. (1986). Characteristics and frequency of malingering among patients with low back pain. *Pain, 25,* 357–364.

Leavitt, S. S., Johnson, T. L., & Beyer, R. D. (1971). The process of recovery: patterns in industrial back injury: Costs and other quantitative measures of effort. *Industrial Medicine & Surgery, 40,* 7.

Lee, K. (1989). *Clinical investigation of the spinal stim system.* Paper presented at the annual meeting of the American Association of Orthopedic Surgeons, Las Vegas, NV.

Lee, N. C., Dicken, R. C., Rubin, G. L., & Ory, H. W. (1984). Confirmation of the preoperative diagnosis for hysterectomy. *American Journal of Obstetrics and Gynecology, 150,* 283–287.

Lefevbre, M. F. (1981). Cognitive distortion and cognitive errors in depressed psychiatric and low back pain patients. *Journal of Consulting and Clinical Psychology, 49,* 517–525.

Levitan, S., Eibschitz, F., deVries, K., & Hakim, M (1985). The value of laparoscopy in women with chronic pelvic pain and a normal pelvis. *International Journal of Obstetrics and Gynecology, 23,* 71.

Lindsay, P., & Wyckoff, M. (1981). The depression-pain and its response to antidepressants. *Psychosomatics, 22,* 571–577.

Little, D. G., & MacDonald, D. (1994). The use of the percentage change in Oswestry Disability Index Score as an outcome measure in lumbar spinal surgery. *Spine, 19*(19), 2139–2134.

Locke, J. J., & Wallace, K. M. (1959). Short-term marital adjustment and prediction tests: Their ability and validity. *Journal of Marriage and Family Living, 21,* 251–255.

Loeser, J. D. (1982). Concepts of pain. In M. Stanton-Hicks & R. Boas (Eds.), *Chronic low back pain.* New York: Raven Press.

Loeser, J. D., Bigos, S. J., Fordyce, W. E., & Violinn, E. P. (1990). Low back pain. In J. J. Bonica (Ed.), *The management of pain* (Vol. 2). Philadelphia: Lee & Febiger.

Long, C. (1981). The relationship between surgical outcome and MMPI profiles in chronic pain patients. *Journal of Clinical Psychology, 37,* 744–749.

Lousberg, R., Schmidt, A. J., & Groenman, N. H. (1992). The relationship between spouse solicitousness and pain behavior: Searching for more evidence. *Pain, 51,* 75–79.

Magni, G., Andreoli, C., de Leo, D., Martinotti, G., & Rossi, C. (1986). Psychological profile of women with chronic pelvic pain. *Archives of Gynecology and Obstetrics, 237,* 165.

Main, C. J., & Spanswick, C. C. (1995). Personality assessment and the Minnesota Multiphasic Personality Inventory. 50 years on: Do we still need our security blanket? *Pain Forum, 4*(2), 90–96.

Manniche, C., Asmussen, K. H., Vinterberg, H., Rose-Hansen, E. B. R., Kramhoft, J., & Jordan, A. (1994). Analysis of preoperative prognostic factors in first-time surgery for lumbar disc herniation, including Finneson's and modified Spengler's score systems. *Danish Medical Bulletin, 41,* 110–115.

Maruta, T., & Osborne, D. (1976). Sexual activity in chronic pain patients. *Psychosomatics, 19,* 531–537.

Massoth, D. L., Dworkin, S. F., Whitney, C. W., Harrison, R. G., Wilson, L., & Turner, J. (1994). Patient explanatory models for temporomandibular disorders. In G. H. Gebhart, D. L. Hammond, & T. S. Jenson (Eds.), *Proceedings of the 7th World Congress on Pain.* Seattle: IASP Press.

Mayer, T. G., Gatchel, R. J., Mayer, H., Kishino, N. D., Keeley, J., & Mooney, V. (1987). A prospective two-year study of functional restoration in industrial low back injury. *Journal of the American Medical Association, 258*(13), 1763–1768.

McCreary, C. P., Clark, G. T., Merril, V., & Oakley, M. A. (1991). Psychological distress and diagnostic subgroups of temporomandibular patients. *Pain, 44*, 29–34.

McDaniel, L. K., Anderson, K. O., Bradley, L. A., Young, L. D., Turner, R A., Agudelo, C. A., & Keefe, F. J. (1986). Development of an observation method for assessing pain behavior in rheumatoid arthritis patients. *Pain, 24*, 165–184.

McMullin, R. (1985). *Handbook of cognitive therapy techniques.* New York: Norton.

Meier, W., Klucken, M, Soyka, D., & Bromm, B. (1993). Hypnotic hypo- and hyperalgesia: divergent effects on pain ratings and pain-related cerebral potentials. *Pain, 53*, 175–182.

Melzack, R. (1975). The McGill Pain Questionnaire: Major properties and scoring methods. *Pain, 1*, 275–299.

Melzack, R., & Dennis, S. G. (1978). Neurophysiological foundations of pain. In R. A. Sternbach (Ed.), *The psychology of pain* (pp. 1–26). New York: Raven Press.

Melzack, R., & Wall, P. D. (1965). Pain mechanisms: A new theory. *Science, 150*, 971–979.

Merskey, H. (1965). The effect of chronic pain upon the response to noxious stimuli by psychiatric patients. *Journal of Psychosomatic Research, 9*, 291–298.

Merskey, H., & Bogduk, N. (Eds.). (1994). *Classification of chronic pain* (2nd ed.). Seattle: IASP Press.

Millstein-Prentky, S., & Olson, R. (1979). Predictability of treatment outcome inpatients with myofascial pain-dysfunction (MPD) syndrome. *Journal of Dental Research, 58*(4), 1341–1346.

Mooney, V. (1990). A randomized double-blind prospective study of the efficacy of pulsed electromagnetic fields for interbody lumbar fusions. *Spine, 15*(7), 708–712.

Nachemson, A. L. (1992). Newest knowledge of low back pain: A critical look. *Clinical, Orthopedic, and Relaxed Research, 279*, 8–20.

National Center for Health Statistics, Pokras, R., & Hufnagel, V. G. (1987). *Hysterectomies in the United States, 1965–1984* (DHHS Publication No. PHS 88–1753). Washington, DC: U.S. Government Printing Office.

National Hospital Discharge Survey, 1990. (1992). *Vital and Health Statistics* (Series 13, No. 112. DHHS Publication No. PHS 88–1753). Washington, DC: U.S. Government Printing Office.

Nolan, T. E., Metheny, M. P., & Smith, R. P. (1992). Unrecognized association of sleep disorders and depression with chronic pelvic pain. *Southern Medical Journal, 85*(12), 1181–1183.

North, R. B. (1995). Neurosurgical approaches to chronic pain. In A. H. White & J. A. Schofferman (Eds.), *Spine care.* St. Louis: Mosby.

North, R. B., Campbell, J. N., James, C. S., Conover-Walker, M. K., Wang, H., Piantadosi, S., Rybock, J. D., & Long, D. M. (1991). Failed back surgery syndr0me: 5-year follow up in 102 patients undergoing repeated operation. *Neurosurgery, 28*(5), 685–691.

O'Leary, A., Shoor, S., Lorig, K., & Holman, H. R. (1988). A cognitive–behavioral treatment for rheumatoid arthritis. *Health Psychology, 7*, 527–544.

Orme, T., Brown, C., & Richardson, H. (1985). The use of the Million Behavioral Health Inventory (MBHI) as a predictor of surgical suitability. In *Proceedings of the International Society for the Study of the Lumbar Spine*. Sydney, Australia.

Othmer, E., & Othmer, S. C. (1991). *The clinical interview: Using DSM–III–R*. Washington D C: American Psychiatric Press.

Pheasant, H. C., Gelbert, D., Goldfarb, J., & Herron, L. (1979). The MMPI as predictor of outcome in low-back surgery. *Spine, 4*(1), 78–84.

Phillips, H. C. (1989) Thoughts provoked by pain. *Behavior Research and Therapy, 27,* 469–473.

Polatin, P. B., Kinney, R. K., Gatchel, R. J., Lillo, E., & Mayer, T. G. (1993). Psychiatric illness and chronic low-back pain. The mind and the spine—which goes first? *Spine, 18,* 66–71.

Rainville, J., Sobel, J., & Hartigan, C. (1995). *Does prior spine surgery affect outcomes of spine rehabilitation for chronic low back pain?* Paper presented at the 10th annual meeting of the North American Spine Society, Washington, DC.

Randolph, C. S., Greene, C. S., Moretti, R., Forbes, D., & Perry, H. T. (1990). Conservative management of temporomandibular disorders: A post treatment comparison between patients from a university clinic and from private practice. *American Journal of Orthodontics & Dentofacial Orthopedics, 98,* 77–82.

Rapkin, A. J., Kames, L. D., Darke, L. L., Sampler, F. M., & Naliboff, B. D. (1990). History of physical and sexual abuse in women with chronic pelvic pain. *Obstetrics and Gynecology, 76*(1), 92–96.

Reiter, R. C. (1990). A profile of women with chronic pelvic pain. *Clinical Obstetrics and Gynecology, 33*(1), 130–136

Reiter, R. C., & Gambone, J. C. (1990). Demographic and historic variables in women with idiopathic chronic pelvic pain. *Obstetrics and Gynecology, 75,* 428–432.

Renaer, M., Vertommen, H., Nijs, P., Wagemans, L., & van Hemelrijck, T. (1979). Psychological aspects of chronic pelvic pain in women. *American Journal of Obstetrics and Gynecology, 134,* 75–80.

Revenson, T., & Felton, B. (1989). Disability and coping as predictors of psychological adjustment to rheumatoid arthritis. *Journal of Consulting and Clinical Psychology, 57*(3), 344–348.

Riley, J. F., Ahern, D. K., & Follick, M. J. (1988). Chronic pain and functional impairment: Assessing beliefs about their relationship. *Archives of Physical and Medical Rehabilitation, 59,* 579–582.

Riley, J. L., Robinson, M. E., Geisser, M. E., Wittmer, V. T., & Smith, A. G. (1995). Relationship between MMPI-2 cluster profiles and surgical outcome in low-back pain patients. *Journal of Spinal Disorders, 8*(3), 213–219.

Roland, M., & Morris, R. (1983). A study of the natural history of back pain. Part I: Development of a reliable and sensitive measure of disability in low-back pain. *Spine, 8,* 141–144.

Romano, J. M., Turner, J. A., & Clancy, S. L. (1989). Sex differences in the relationship of pain patient dysfunction to spouse adjustment. *Pain, 39,* 289–296.

Rosensteil, A. K., & Keefe, F. J. (1983). The use of coping strategies in chronic low back pain patients: Relationship to patient characteristics and current adjustment. *Pain, 17,* 33–44.

Rosenthal, R. H., Ling, F. W., Rosenthal, T. L., & McNeeley, S. G. (1984).Chronic pelvic pain: Psychological features and laparoscopic findings. *Psychosomatics, 25*(11), 833–841.

Rossi, E. L., Ryan, M. O., & Sharp, F. A. (Eds.). (1983). *Healing in hypnosis: The seminars, workshops, and lectures of Milton Erickson* (Vol. 1). New York: Irving.

Rudy, T. E., Kerns, R. D., & Turk, D. C. (1988). Chronic pain and depression: Toward a cognitive–behavioral mediation model. *Pain, 35,* 129–140.

Rugh, J. D., & Solberg, W. K., (1985). Oral health status in the United States: Temporomandibular disorders. *Journal of Dental Education, 49,* 398–405.

Ryan, M. M., Dennerstein, L., & Pepperell, R. (1989). Psychological aspects of hysterectomy: A prospective study. *British Journal of Psychiatry, 154,* 516–522.

Sacerdote, P. (1982). Techniques of hypnotic intervention with pain patients. In J. Barber & C. Adrian (Eds.), *Psychological approaches to the management of pain* (pp. 60–83). New York: Brunner/Mazel.

Schiffman, E., Fricton, J. R., Haley, D., & Shapiro, B. L. (1989). The prevalence and treatment needs of subjects with temporomandibular disorders. *Journal of the American Dental Association, 120,* 295–304.

Schmidt, A. (1987). The behavioral management of pain: A criticism of a response. *Pain, 30,* 285–291.

Schmidt, A. J. M., & Brands, A. E. F. (1986). Persistence behavior of chronic low back pain patients in an acute pain situation. *Journal of Psychosomatic Research, 30,* 339–346.

Schofferman, J. (1995). Diagnostic decision making. In A. H. White & J. A. Schofferman (Eds.), *Spine care.* St. Louis: Mosby.

Schofferman, J., Anderson, D., Hinds, R., Smith, G., & White, A. (1992). Childhood psychological trauma correlates with unsuccessful lumbar spine surgery. *Spine, 17* (Suppl. 6), S138–S1384.

Schwartz, L., Slater, M. A., Birchler, G. R., & Atkinson, J. H. (1991). Depression in spouses of chronic pain patients: The role of patient pain and anger, and marital satisfaction. *Pain, 44,* 61–68.

Schwartz, R. A., Greene, C. S., & Laskin, D. M. (1979). Personality characteristics of patients with myofascial pain-dysfunction (MPD) syndrome unresponsive to conventional therapy. *Journal of Dental Research, 58,* 1435–1439.

Seligman, M. E. P. (1975). *Helplessness: On depression, development, and death.* San Francisco: Freeman.

Seligman, M. E. P. (1976). Learned helplessness and depression in animals and men. In J. T. Spence, R. C. Carson, & J. W. Thibaut (Eds.), *Behavioral approaches to therapy.* Morristown, NJ: General Learning Press.

Shutty, M. S., & DeGood, D. E. (1987). Cluster analyses of responses of low-back pain patients to the SCL-90: Comparison of empirical versus derived subscales. *Rehabilitation Psychology, 32,* 133–143.

Sifneos, P. E. (1987). *Short-term dynamic psychotherapy: Evaluation and technique* (2nd ed.). New York: Plenum Medical.

Skevington, S. M. (1993). Chronic pain and depression: Universal or personal helplessness? *Pain, 15,* 309–317.

Skinner, B. F. (1938). *The behavior of organisms: An experimental approach.* New York: Appleton-Century-Crofts.

Skinner, B. F. (1974). *About behaviorism.* New York: Alfred A. Knopf.

Slocumb, J. C. (1990a). Chronic somatic, myofascial, and neurogenic abdominal pelvic pain. *Clinical Obstetrics and Gynecology, 33*(1), 145–153.

Slocumb, J. C. (1990b). Operative management of chronic abdominal pelvic pain. *Clinical Obstetrics and Gynecology, 33*(1), 196–204.

Smith, W. L., & Duerksen, D. L. (1979). Personality and the relief of chronic pain: Predicting surgical outcome. *Clinical Neuropsychology, 1.*

Sorenson, L. V. (1992). Preoperative psychological testing with the MMPI at first operation for prolapsed lumbar disc. *Danish Medical Bulletin, 39,* 186–190.

Sorenson, L. V., & Mors, O. (1988). Presentation of a new MMPI scale to predict outcome after first lumbar diskectomy. *Pain, 34,* 191–194.

Spengler, D. M., Freeman, C., Westbrook, R., & Miller, J. W. (1980). Low-back pain following multiple lumbar spine procedures: Failure of initial selection? *Spine, 5*(4), 356–360.

Spengler, D. M., Ouelette, E. A., Battie, M., & Zeh, J. (1990). Elective discectomy for herniation of a lumbar disc. *Journal of Bone and Joint Surgery (America), 12,* 230–237.

Spitzer, W. O. (1987). Scientific approach to the assessment and management of activity-related spinal disorders. *Spine, 12* (Suppl.), 1.

Stauffer, R. N., & Coventry, M. B. (1972). Anterior interbody lumbar spine fusion: Analysis of Mayo Clinic series. *Journal of Bone and Joint Surgery (America), 54,* 756–789.

Steege, J. F., & Stout, A. L. (1991). Resolution of chronic pelvic pain after laparoscopic lysis of lesions. *American Journal of Obstetrics and Gynecology, 165,* 278–283.

Stewards, L., Saltier, M. S., Brittle, G. R., et al. (1991). Depression in spouses of chronic pain patients: The role of patient pain and anger, and marital satisfaction. *Pain, 44,* 61–68.

Stewards, R. A., Greene, C. S., & Alaskan, D. M. (1979). Personality characteristics of patients with myofascial pain-dysfunction (MPD) syndrome unresponsive to conventional therapy. *Journal of Dental Research, 58*(5), 1435–1439.

Stovall, T. G., Ling, F. W., & Crawford, D. A. (1990). Hysterectomy for chronic pelvic pain of presumed uterine etiology. *Obstetrics and Gynecology, 75,* 676–679.

Taylor, V. M., Deyo, R. A., Cherkin, D. C., & Kreuter, W. (1994). Low back pain hospitalization: Recent United States trends and regional variations. *Spine, 19,* 1207–1212.

Ter Kuile, M. M., Spinhoven, P., Linssen, C. G., Zitman, F. G., Van Dyck, R., & Rooijmans, G. M. (1994). Autogenic training and cognitive self-hypnosis for the treatment of recurrent headaches in three different subject groups. *Pain, 58,* 331–340.

Texas Worker's Compensation Commission (1995, January 6). Mental health treatment guidelines. *Texas Register,* 1–80.

Tollison, C. D. (Ed.). (1989). *Handbook of chronic pain management.* Baltimore: Williams & Wilkins.

Turk, D. C., & Fernandez, E. (1995). Personality assessment and the Minnesota Multiphasic Personality Inventory in chronic pain: Underdeveloped and overexposed. *Pain Forum, 4*(2), 104–107.

Turk, D. C., & Rudy, T. E. (1988). Toward an empirically driven taxonomy of chronic pain patients: Integration of psychological assessment data. *Journal of Consulting and Clinical Psychology, 56* (2), 233–238.

Turner, J. A., & Clancy, S. (1986). Strategies for coping with chronic low back pain: Relationship to pain and disability. *Pain, 24,* 355–364.

Turner, J. A., & Denny, M. C. (1993). Do antidepressant medications relieve chronic low back pain? *Journal of Family Practice, 37*(6), 545–553.

Turner, J. A., Ersek, M., Herron, L., Haselkorn, J., Kent, D., Ciol, Marcia, A., & Deyo, R. (1992). Patient outcomes after lumbar spinal fusions. *Journal of the American Medical Association, 268*(7), 907–911.

Turner, J. A., Herron, L. & Weiner, P. (1986). Utility of the MMPI pain assessment index in predicting outcome after lumbar surgery. *Journal of Clinical Psychology, 42*, 764–769.

Turner, J. A., & Jensen, M. P. (1993). Efficacy of cognitive therapy for chronic low back pain. *Pain, 52*, 169–177.

Uomoto, J. M., Turner, J. A., & Herron, L. D. (1988). Use of the MMPI and MCMI in predicting outcome of lumbar laminectomy. *Journal of Clinical Psychology, 44*, 191–197.

Vanharanta, H., Sachs, B. L., Spivey, M. A., Guyer, R. D., Hochschuler, S. H., Rashbaum, R. F., Johnson, R. G., Ohnmeiss, D., & Mooney, V. (1987). The relationship of pain provocation to lumbar disc deterioration as seen by CT/discography. *Spine, 12*, 295–298.

Von Korff, M., Dworkin, S. F., & LeResche, L. (1990). Graded chronic pain status: An epidemiologic evaluation. *Pain, 40*, 279–291.

Waddell, G. (1987). A new clinical model for the treatment of low-back pain. *Spine, 12*(7), 632–644.

Waddell, G., McCulloch, J. A., Kummel, E., & Venner, R. M. (1980). Nonorganic physical signs in low-back pain. *Spine, 5*(2), 117–125.

Waddell, G., Newton, M., Henderson, I., Somerville, D., & Main, C. J. (1993). A Fear-Avoidance Beliefs Questionnaire (FABQ) and the role of fear-avoidance beliefs in chronic low back pain and disability. *Pain, 52*, 157–168.

Wadden, T. A., Foster, G. D., & Letizia, K. A. (1994). One-year behavioral treatment of obesity: Comparison of moderate and severe caloric restriction and the effects of weight maintenance therapy. *Journal of Consulting and Clinical Psychology, 62*, 165–171.

Walker, E., Katon, W., Harrop-Griffiths, J., Holm, L., Russo, J., & Hickok, L. R. (1988). Relationship of chronic pelvic pain to psychiatric diagnoses and childhood sexual abuse. *American Journal of Psychiatry, 145*, 75–80.

Walker, E., Katon, W., Neraas, K., Jemelka, R. P., & Massoth, D. (1992). Dissociation in women with chronic pelvic pain. *American Journal of Psychiatry, 149*, 534.

Walker, S., & Cousins, M. J. (1994). Failed back surgery syndrome. *Australian Family Physician, 23*, 2308–2314.

Wallston, F. A., Wallston, B. S., & DeVellis, R. (1978). Development of the Multidimensional Health Locus of Control (MHLC) scales. *Health Education Monograph, 6*, 160–170. Washington DC: American Psychiatric Press.

Weber, H. (1983). Lumbar disc herniation: A controlled perspective study with ten years of observation. *Spine, 8*, 131–140.

White, A. H., & Schofferman, J. A. (Eds.). (1995). *Spine care*. St. Louis: Mosby.

Whitehead, W. E . (1993). Behavioral medicine approaches to gastrointestinal disorders. *Journal of Consulting and Clinical Psychology, 60*(4), 605–612.

Wiesel, S. W., Tsourmas, N., Feffer, H. L., Citrin, C. M., & Patronas, N. (1984). A study of computer-assisted tomography I. The incidence of positive CAT scans in an asymptomatic group of patients. *Spine, 9*, 549–551.

Williams, D. A., Urban, B., Keefe, F. J., Shutty, M. S., & France, R. (1995). Cluster analyses of pain patients' responses to the SCL-90R. *Pain, 61*, 81–91.

Wiltse, L. L., & Rocchio, P. D. (1975). Preoperative psychological tests as predictors of success of chemonucleolysis in the treatment of low-back syndrome. *Journal of Bone and Joint Surgery (America), 75,* 478–483.

Wood, D. P., Wood, M. G., & Reiter, R. C. (1990). Psychogenic chronic pelvic pain: Diagnosis and management. *Clinical Obstetrics and Gynecologia, 33*(1), 189–195.

Wright, M. E., & Wright, B. A. (1987). *Clinical practice of hypnotherapy.* New York: Guilford.

Zung, W. (1965). A self-rating depression scale. *Archives of General Psychiatry, 12,* 63–70.

Author Index

Subject Index

improving, 12
predicting, 14, 67, 77, 80
Oversensitivity to pain (see perception, pain, excessive)

P

Pain
definitions of, 16
experimental, 22, 71–72, 73
functional, 19, 21
interdisciplinary programs for (see pain centers and programs)
organic, 18, 19, 21
perception (see perception, pain)
psychogenic, 17, 18, 19
Pain behaviors (see behavior, pain)
Pain centers and programs, 20, 21, 25, 99, 100, 107, 120
Pain control techniques, 148
Pain generator, 4, 31, 37, 38, 42
Pain modification tests (see diagnostic tests and procedures)
Pain sensitivity (see perception, pain, excessive)
Pain signals (see nociception)
Pathophysiology, underlying pain syndromes, 8, 23, 55, 85, 143, 144
Patient
preparing for referral, 29
handouts, 30
Perception
of pain, 18, 21–23, 26, 36, 62, 63, 124, 130, 132
excessive, 21, 26, 38, 71, 104, 116, 120, 136, 140, 146
of physical capabilities, 85
Pelvic pain, chronic, 131–137
epidemiology of, 131–132
hysterectomy for, 131–132
indications for, 131
idiopathic,
definition of, 131–132
PPS in, 3, 131–137
risk factors associated with, 133–135
Personality
definition of, 68
tests, 68–78
Physical abuse (see abuse, physical)
Plans, treatment (see treatment plans)

Praise, as a reward for well behavior, 20, 21, 106
Presurgical psychological screening (PPS),
definition of, 2
goals of, 3, 6, 49
high-risk threshold, 11, 92, 93, 94–96, 107, 147
comparing total risk to, 11, 93, 94–96, 147
rules for altering, 94–96
medical risk factors in, 41–46
models, 10–12, 93
for general chronic pain conditions, 141–148
for spine surgery, 93
outcome categories in (see outcome categories)
prognoses resulting from (see prognosis)
psychological risk factors in (see risk factors, psychological)
referral criteria for 29–30
reports, 7
scales (PPS Scale), 90–96, 110
general, 143
in spine surgery 90–96
written summary, 121
Problematic behaviors
determining effect on surgical prognosis, 95–96, 147–148
identifying, 95–96
Prognosis
surgical, 12–14, 48, 117, 148
determination of, 6, 11–12, 89–96, 147
Psychiatric hospitalization, 95
Psychoanalysis (see theories, psychoanalytic)
Psychogenic pain, 17–19
Psychometric tests (see tests, psychometric)
Psychosis
as a red flag, 14

R

Rapport, 47, 54, 62
importance of developing, 49
influence on decision making, 12, 47